OPPOSING
VIEWPOINTS®
SERIES

Crime and Criminals

Other Books of Related Interest:

Opposing Viewpoints Series

Criminal Justice

Mandatory Sentencing

White-Collar Crime

Current Controversies Series

Guns and Violence

Prisons

At Issue Series

Is Gun Ownership a Right?

Mental Illness and Criminal Behavior

Piracy on the High Seas

"Congress shall make
no law ... abridging
the freedom of speech,
or of the press."

First Amendment to the U.S. Constitution

The basic foundation of our democracy is the First Amendment guarantee of freedom of expression. The Opposing Viewpoints Series is dedicated to the concept of this basic freedom and the idea that it is more important to practice it than to enshrine it.

**OPPOSING
VIEWPOINTS®
SERIES**

Crime and Criminals

Christina Fisanick, Book Editor

GREENHAVEN PRESS
A part of Gale, Cengage Learning

GALE
CENGAGE Learning™

Detroit • New York • San Francisco • New Haven, Conn • Waterville, Maine • London

Christine Nasso, *Publisher*
Elizabeth Des Chenes, *Managing Editor*

© 2010 Greenhaven Press, a part of Gale, Cengage Learning.

Gale and Greenhaven Press are registered trademarks used herein under license.

For more information, contact:
Greenhaven Press
27500 Drake Rd.
Farmington Hills, MI 48331-3535
Or you can visit our Internet site at gale.cengage.com

For product information and technology assistance, contact us at

Gale Customer Support, 1-800-877-4253
For permission to use material from this text or product, submit all requests online at www.cengage.com/permissions

Further permissions questions can be emailed to permissionrequest@cengage.com

Articles in Greenhaven Press anthologies are often edited for length to meet page requirements. In addition, original titles of these works are changed to clearly present the main thesis and to explicitly indicate the author's opinion. Every effort is made to ensure that Greenhaven Press accurately reflects the original intent of the authors. Every effort has been made to trace the owners of copyrighted material.

Cover photograph © ryasick photography.

LIBRARY OF CONGRESS CATALOGING-IN-PUBLICATION DATA

Crime and criminals / Christina Fisanick, book editor.
    p. cm. -- (Opposing viewpoints)
    Includes bibliographical references and index.
    978-0-7377-4360-9 (hardcover)
    978-0-7377-4359-3 (pbk.)
    1. Crime--United States. 2. Criminals--United States. 3. Crime prevention--United States. 4. Criminal justice, Administration of--United States. 5. Recidivism--United States. I. Fisanick, Christina.
    HV6789.C68133 2009
    364.973--dc22

                         2009021918

Printed in the United States of America
1 2 3 4 5 6 7 13 12 11 10 09

Contents

Chapter 3: How Can Crime Be Prevented?

Chapter 4: How Can Recidivism Rates Be Reduced?

Why Consider Opposing Viewpoints?

> *"The only way in which a human being can make some approach to knowing the whole of a subject is by hearing what can be said about it by persons of every variety of opinion and studying all modes in which it can be looked at by every character of mind. No wise man ever acquired his wisdom in any mode but this."*
>
> *John Stuart Mill*

In our media-intensive culture it is not difficult to find differing opinions. Thousands of newspapers and magazines and dozens of radio and television talk shows resound with differing points of view. The difficulty lies in deciding which opinion to agree with and which "experts" seem the most credible. The more inundated we become with differing opinions and claims, the more essential it is to hone critical reading and thinking skills to evaluate these ideas. Opposing Viewpoints books address this problem directly by presenting stimulating debates that can be used to enhance and teach these skills. The varied opinions contained in each book examine many different aspects of a single issue. While examining these conveniently edited opposing views, readers can develop critical thinking skills such as the ability to compare and contrast authors' credibility, facts, argumentation styles, use of persuasive techniques, and other stylistic tools. In short, the Opposing Viewpoints Series is an ideal way to attain the higher-level thinking and reading skills so essential in a culture of diverse and contradictory opinions.

In addition to providing a tool for critical thinking, Opposing Viewpoints books challenge readers to question their own strongly held opinions and assumptions. Most people form their opinions on the basis of upbringing, peer pressure, and personal, cultural, or professional bias. By reading carefully balanced opposing views, readers must directly confront new ideas as well as the opinions of those with whom they disagree. This is not to simplistically argue that everyone who reads opposing views will—or should—change his or her opinion. Instead, the series enhances readers' understanding of their own views by encouraging confrontation with opposing ideas. Careful examination of others' views can lead to the readers' understanding of the logical inconsistencies in their own opinions, perspective on why they hold an opinion, and the consideration of the possibility that their opinion requires further evaluation.

Evaluating Other Opinions

To ensure that this type of examination occurs, Opposing Viewpoints books present all types of opinions. Prominent spokespeople on different sides of each issue as well as well-known professionals from many disciplines challenge the reader. An additional goal of the series is to provide a forum for other, less known, or even unpopular viewpoints. The opinion of an ordinary person who has had to make the decision to cut off life support from a terminally ill relative, for example, may be just as valuable and provide just as much insight as a medical ethicist's professional opinion. The editors have two additional purposes in including these less known views. One, the editors encourage readers to respect others' opinions—even when not enhanced by professional credibility. It is only by reading or listening to and objectively evaluating others' ideas that one can determine whether they are worthy of consideration. Two, the inclusion of such viewpoints encourages the important critical thinking skill of objectively evaluating an author's credentials and bias. This evaluation will illuminate an author's reasons for taking a particular stance on an issue and will aid in readers' evaluation of the author's ideas.

It is our hope that these books will give readers a deeper understanding of the issues debated and an appreciation of the complexity of even seemingly simple issues when good and honest people disagree. This awareness is particularly important in a democratic society such as ours in which people enter into public debate to determine the common good. Those with whom one disagrees should not be regarded as enemies but rather as people whose views deserve careful examination and may shed light on one's own.

Thomas Jefferson once said that "difference of opinion leads to inquiry, and inquiry to truth." Jefferson, a broadly educated man, argued that "if a nation expects to be ignorant and free . . . it expects what never was and never will be." As individuals and as a nation, it is imperative that we consider the opinions of others and examine them with skill and discernment. The Opposing Viewpoints Series is intended to help readers achieve this goal.

David L. Bender and Bruno Leone,
Founders

Introduction

"We sacrifice precious community resources to maintain a prison system that
creates instability, ill health and disease,
while failing to keep us safe."

Donna Willmott,
Family Advocacy Coordinator at
Legal Services for Prisoners with Children

According to an April 2008 report by the International Centre for Prison Studies at King's College London, the United States leads the world in prison population at 2.3 million criminals behind bars. China, which has four times the general population of the United States, comes in second with 1.6 million citizens locked up. As a result, American prisons are overcrowded, and the prison industry is one of the fastest growing sectors of the economy. Criminologists continue to search for answers to overcrowding, while state and local officials struggle with how best to house criminals when their budgets are already being stretched by a downturned economy.

Multiple reasons have been cited for why American prisons house nearly a quarter of the world's prisoners. Researchers cite American morality, the war on drugs, and a broken social system that cannot care for displaced citizens. Tough sentencing laws are the most frequently referenced. California made history in 1994 when it passed the Three Strikes and You're Out law, which mandates a sentence of twenty-five years to life in prison for third-time felons. Fifteen years later, supporters of the law argue that it has been effective in reducing crime. Mike Reynolds, who pushed forward the Three Strikes and You're Out law following the murder of his daughter, notes on his Web site www.threestrikes.org that in the fifteen years since the law was passed, "an average of 1 million serious or violent crimes have been prevented every five years and ten thousand Californians have been spared from becoming murder victims." In other words, although this law contributes to the growing prison population, it has been effective in keeping criminals off the streets and innocent people out of harm's way.

Not everyone agrees that tougher sentencing keeps Americans safe. Organizations concerned about the fairness of the law point to judges who do not always follow the mandate, to racial biases in the justice system, and that the punishment often does not fit the crime. In November 2008, Families to Amend California's Three Strikes (FACTS) attempted to get legislation passed that would revise the law and limit injustices. Seeing the Three Strikes and You're Out law as unjust, they proposed the following changes:

- make three strikes applicable only to violent felonies;

- count only crimes committed after the law's passage in 1994 as strikes;

- treat multiple counts committed during a single act as only one strike;

- secure a "wash-out" period whereby convictions older than ten years don't count as strikes;

- exclude burglary of unoccupied dwellings from the list of strikeable offenses;

- exclude juvenile offenses from three strikes provisions. Their proposition, however, did not gain enough support, and their fight continues. According to a recent issue of their newsletter, *The Striker*, they "will not stop until this law is history."

Regardless of why America's prisons are overcrowded, the corrections system must find ways to house criminals. According to a 2008 report by the International Centre for Prison

Studies, America's prison population is 107 percent of its official capacity, which means that prison conditions are less than desirable. Penal Reform International argues in a July 2007 report that "overcrowding undermines the ability of prison systems to meet the basic needs of prisoners, such as health care, food, and accommodation. It also compromises the provision of rehabilitation programmes, educational training, and recreational activities." Even if state governments have the money to build new prisons, they cannot be built fast enough to accommodate the growing population.

Although many solutions to prison overcrowding have been proposed, interstate prisoner transfer has prompted the most controversy. Governors in states across the nation have opted to transfer prisoners to other states when their own facilities have exceeded maximum capacity. In defense of his 2006 declaration to allow prisoner transfer, California Governor Arnold Schwarzenegger announced that "these actions are necessary to protect the safety and well-being of the officers, inmates, and the public." Proponents of prisoner transfer programs argue that it is a win-win situation. It costs the transferring state less money to ship inmates to other locations, and states with empty beds make a profit.

Opponents of prisoner transfer programs argue that this method of reducing and redistributing the prison population does far more harm than good. For example, by moving prisoners out of their home states, many of them are unable to see their friends and relatives. David Fathi of the American Civil Liberties Union's National Prison Project in Washington, D.C., notes in the May 2006 issue of *In These Times* that in these cases "visitation is all but impossible, and visitations are very important to prisoner mental health. [Visits] are usually correlated with positive prison adjustment behavior as well as decreased recidivism [return to prison] rates." This is especially true for prisoners who are moved long distances, such as the case with several female inmates from Hawaii who are currently housed in a Kentucky facility. According to *In These Times* reporter Silja J.A. Talvi in May 2006, "Those who have long sentences may never see their families or home states again."

Finding a solution to America's overburdened prison system is essential to the well-being of sentenced criminals and the public at large. The authors in *Opposing Viewpoints: Crime and Criminals* debate current views on ways of dealing with those persons who break the law in the following chapters: "Are All Criminals Treated Fairly?" "Should Some Criminals Be Treated Differently?" "How Can Crime Be Prevented?" and "How Can Recidivism Rates Be Reduced?" In the end, the biggest challenge is determining how best to fight crime while preserving the dignity of those who commit it.

OPPOSING
VIEWPOINTS®
SERIES

CHAPTER 1

Are All Criminals Treated Fairly?

Chapter Preface

The number of women in prison has soared in recent years. According to the Bureau of Justice Statistics, the rate of women being incarcerated has nearly doubled the percentage increase of men during the same period. With the rise has come a host of problems, including availability of women-only prison facilities and an adequate number of properly trained female prison guards. As a result, pregnancy has become a complication and determining how best to handle the situation is a considerable challenge. Most recently, the use of shackles during childbirth has been at the forefront of the debate.

It is common for female prisoners to be shackled while giving birth. Currently, only two U.S. states, Illinois and California, have specific policies forbidding the use of restraints on birthing prisoners. Prison and government officials routinely support this practice by citing the possibility of escape. England's former prisons minister [Anne Widdecombe] argued in a January 1996 article in *The Independent* that prisoners should be shackled during childbirth. "Some MPs [Members of Parliament] may like to think that a pregnant woman would not or could not escape. Unfortunately, this is not true. The fact is that hospitals are not secure places in which to keep prisoners, and since 1990, twenty women have escaped from hospitals." Her sentiments have been echoed in the United States and other countries around the world, as concerns for the general public often trump the comfort of inmates.

Not everyone agrees. A March 2006 article in the *New York Times* set off a firestorm of debate about this practice. According to the author, Adam Liptak, "Despite sporadic complaints and occasional lawsuits, the practice of shackling prisoners in labor continues to be relatively common." He cites multiple instances of prisoners being restrained throughout the laboring process, including the delivery. Opponents of this practice argue that it is harmful to both mother and baby. According to the American College of Obstetricians in June 2007, "Physical restraints have interfered with the ability of physicians to safely practice medicine by reducing their ability to assess and evaluate the physical condition of the mother and the fetus, and have similarly made the labor and delivery process more difficult than it needs to be; thus, overall putting the health and lives of the women and unborn children at risk." They further note that because an armed guard is present with the laboring mother at all times that these restraints are not even necessary.

Finding a balance between protecting law-abiding citizens and preserving the basic human rights of criminals will remain a constant challenge. The authors in this chapter take up this debate by exploring the treatment of men, women, and minorities who break the law. As the number of women inmates continues to rise, the challenges of pregnancy and childbirth behind bars will become more problematic.

"If a woman is at fault there is a great closing of eyes and opening of hearts— legality be damned."

Men Suffer More Discrimination by the Judicial System than Women

Richard F. Doyle

Richard F. Doyle is a writer and lecturer who focuses on men's rights, especially in the context of divorce. He has written several books including The Rape of Men *and* Save the Males, *from which the following viewpoint is excerpted. He argues that men are treated more harshly by the justice system because of gender bias in favor of women. Citing examples that range from child abuse to prostitution, he claims that women serve less time than men for committing the same crimes.*

As you read, consider the following questions:

1. How many more times are men arrested than women?

2. What percentage of homicides in the United States are committed by women?

Richard F. Doyle, *Save the Males: Masculinity and Men's Rights Redux*. Forest Lake, MN: Poor Richard's Press, 2008. Copyright © 2008 Richard Doyle. Reproduced by permission of the author.

3. Between 1930 and 1995, how many men and how many women were executed?

It is a basic principle of law that a person is presumed innocent until proven guilty. However there is an *a priori* presumption to the contrary regarding males; nearly every cop in the country lives for the opportunity to rescue damsels in distress from predicaments with men, and prosecutors are frothing to convict. Innocence is no defense.

On the other hand, if a woman is at fault there is a great closing of eyes and opening of hearts—legality be damned. Women are favored from decision to arrest, to amount of bail required, to guilt or innocence in judgment, to severity of sentence, to physical conditions of imprisonment, to release on parole. Women are charged fewer times than men for violent crime, convicted less when guilty of the same crimes as men, and are given shorter sentences or simply receive probation. Judges are reluctant to jail women; while men are arrested 4 times as often as women, they are imprisoned 24 times as often.

A substantial percentage of all convicted male prisoners are actually innocent, scapegoated victims of ambitious, man-hating or Feminist-pandering prosecutors or judges. This large number attests to the blatant indifference toward justice for men, and the haste of prosecutors, judges and juries to convict men merely because of their sex. . . .

Mark Wayne Rathbun raped 14 women around Long Beach, California, from 1997 to 2002. None died or were seriously physically harmed according to newspaper accounts. In September 2004 he was sentenced to 1,030 years plus 10 life terms. Contrast that with the sentences given Andrea Yates and Susan Smith for *murder* of their children by drowning (Yates—5 children, Smith—2). They each got one life sentence and, as everyone knows, will be home in a few years. Incredibly enough, on January 6, 2005, a 3-judge Appeals Court panel overturned Yates' conviction because the prosecution's psychiatrist was confused regarding an episode of TV's *Law & Order*. Out on bail, she will get a new trial or be allowed to plead down. Both Andrea's husband and Susan's ex-husband chivalrously ran to their defense.

Gender Imbalance

Society has lost its sense of proportion. A woman can murder a man and receive less punishment than a man who cannot pay his alimony or who urinates in the street. Women who kill their spouse, even while not in immanent and immediate danger, need only murmur "brutality" and hearts begin bleeding. No rebuttal is possible; the victim is dead. It happens so often I no longer keep files on it. . . .

Jilted actress Claudine Longet, who killed live-in lover Spider Sabitch because he found a new girlfriend, was convicted and sentenced to 30 days, the same sentence a young Wisconsin lad served in 1984 for playing hooky, and a Cheyenne, Wyo., man for violating a local ordinance by fishing with a worm instead of a fly. She served the time at her convenience in a specially redecorated cell. . . .

Acquittal, token punishment or forgiveness of women who murder and maim men signals open season on men. This is a license to kill. Women premeditate over half of the domestic murders they commit, and yet half of them claim self-defense quite successfully. They are convicted of between 15 and 26 percent of the homicides in this country, but suffer less than 1 percent of the executions, proportionately 50 times less than men in relation to their murder conviction rate. Between 1930 and 1995, 3,313 males have been executed and only 30 females.

Men are assumed to deserve capital punishment and death because they are perceived to have less value than women. Thirty six states and the Federal government have the death penalty. While that penalty is eminently appropriate in many cases, because of the haste to condemn males to death perhaps it ought to be suspended unless and until justice prevails. Admittedly though, in recent years the lengthy appeals process has greatly minimized chances of executing the innocent.

In battered baby cases, guilty fathers are fined heavily or jailed. Mothers, guilty of more and worse cruelty, are usually put on probation and ordered to get psychiatric help. In other words, if the father does it, he's a criminal: if the mother does it, she is mentally ill and needs help.

Alba Ingrid Scarpelli, of Germantown, Alabama, was convicted of multiple counts of child abuse for tying up and torturing her 5-year-old son, Richard. Her sentence? 18 months on work release. The boy's father, Alan Lee Holmes, merely stood by while girlfriend Scarpelli committed the abuse. His sentence? *eight years* in prison. She does the crime; he does the time. . . .

In Will County, Illinois, near Chicago, forty-four-year-old Fred M. Flynn and his thirty-four-year-old wife, Rita, were convicted of selling their twelve-year-old daughter in 1972 for marriage to a wealthy man for $28,000. Although they both pled guilty to the identical charge, the man got a five-month jail sentence and the wife got probation. . . .

Blaming Males

In October of 2005 Lynndie England of Abu Ghraib [U.S. prison in Iraq] fame was sentenced to 3 years for mistreating prisoners. Her equally guilty male co-operative, Pvt. Charles Graner Jr., is serving 10 years in Leavenworth.

Male defenders of U.S. borders are treated more harshly than a female saboteur. Border agents Ignacio Ramos and Jose Alanso Compean shot and slightly wounded a drug smuggler fleeing back across the Mexican border. They were sentenced to 11 and 12 years respectively, despite their claim of self-defense. A woman in their shoes probably would have been

Sentenced Prisoners, 2000–2006

Characteristics	2000	2005	2006
Total	1,321,100	1,461,100	1,502,200
Male	1,237,500	1,362,500	1,399,100
White	398,800	459,700	478,000
Black or African-American	528,300	547,200	534,200
Hispanic or Latino	240,700	279,000	290,500
Female	83,700	98,600	103,100
White	33,300	45,800	49,100
Black or African-American	32,000	29,900	28,600
Hispanic or Latino	13,000	15,900	17,500
Percent of sentenced prisoners	100%	100%	100%
Male	93.7%	93.3%	93.1%
White	30.2	31.4	31.8
Black or African-American	40.0	37.5	35.6
Hispanic or Latino	18.2	19.1	19.3
Female	6.3%	6.7%	6.9%
White	2.5	3.1	3.3
Black or African-American	2.4	2.0	1.9
Hispanic or Latino	1.0	1.1	1.2

Note: Data are for prisoners sentenced to more than 1 year.

TAKEN FROM: U.S. Department of Justice, "Prisoners in 2006," *Bureau of Justice Statistics Bulletin*, December 2007.

hailed as a hero. In the same week, attorney Lynne Stewart, who smuggled messages from imprisoned terrorist Sheik Omar Abdel Rahman to his co-conspirators in Egypt, had her wrist slapped with a 28 month sentence.

Practically every time a man and woman get into a physical fight, regardless of who is the aggressor, the man is blamed. If married, police usually throw him out of his house. As 17-year Seattle family law attorney Lisa Scott explains, "From top to bottom the current domestic violence system won't let women be anything but victims and can't see men as anything but batterers. And from the moment a 911 call is made there is practically no such thing as an innocent man. It doesn't matter that you're actually innocent. Or that she attacked you first. Or that you both went over the line and that both of you want to put it behind you and work it out. The system will prosecute you and persecute you until you've confessed your sins—even if you've none to confess. And you're not cured until they say you're cured—even if you were never sick to begin with."

If a man is caught looking into a home in which a woman is undressing, he will be arrested for voyeurism. If a woman is looking, again the man will be arrested; this time for indecent exposure. It happened; the Mississippi Supreme Court rationalized the verdict, as did courts in Delaware County, Pennsylvania and Portsmouth, Virginia. There are hundreds of such cases. In Texas a man and woman violated a local ordinance by swimming in the nude. Police arrested only the man. . . .

Double Standards

Prostitution is another example of the double standard. It is the only transgression in which the buyers of an illegal commodity are considered as culpable as the sellers, or more so, because they are men. One might expect the prostitute to be a more socially undesirable creature than her customer; evidently not. In Sweden (does this surprise you?) the clients of prostitutes are prosecuted, but the prostitutes are not. Extending the logic of this nonsense makes buyers of stolen goods and of drugs as culpable as the fences and pushers, which might rationalize the consideration by prosecutors and the media that Rush Limbaugh [the talk radio host who admitted prescription drug addiction] was more culpable than his female supplier.

Police officers around the country dress as women or use policewomen to entrap men, then arrest those who respond. Yet a man who with a detective watched his wife have intercourse with another man was denied a divorce on grounds of adultery because of "entrapment." The court rationalized he could have stopped her (It might be interesting to attempt citizen's arrests of policewomen shills for soliciting). In a 15 month study, men were defendants in 63 percent of prostitution cases prosecuted by the St. Paul, Minnesota, City Attorney's Office. Ponder this convoluted logic: some years ago Minnesota prostitution laws were held unconstitutional by Judges Ledbodott and Riley because they discriminate against women. Yet laws which explicitly punish only males for nonsupport have been held to be constitutional. . . .

If a man kills a fetus against the mother's will he has murdered a human being. If her abortionist does it, it's her "right" and the fetus loses human status, even if already 4/5ths out of her body. A glaring, example of this is the conviction and life sentence of 18-year-old Gerardo Flores of Lufkin, Texas. His pregnant 16-year-old girlfriend, Erica Basoria, tried unsuccessfully to induce miscarriage then asked Gerardo to kick her in the stomach, causing the death of their twins. The equally guilty Basoria was not charged. Another example is the murder of Laci Peterson and her unborn son, Connor. Her husband Scott was convicted of killing both, of 1st degree murder of Laci and of 2nd degree murder of Connor. He received the death penalty. Yet she and an abortionist could have killed Connor without danger of conviction. Woman who damage their babies during pregnancy by fouling their bodies with poisons (nicotine, alcohol, dope, etc.) are seldom prosecuted.

If these were unusual situations, I would have little reason to write about crime and punishment, and could stick to my original concern about anti-male discrimination in divorce, which is more prevalent if not more shocking. But the plight of such men isn't unusual. Similar outrages are happening in courts across our land every day. If the objects of this pogrom were women, or even real criminals, any number of individuals and organizations would be loudly defending and inventing their rights and stretching the Constitution incredibly to protect same.

> "The unequal playing field that plagued an incarcerated woman before her arrest follows her through the criminal justice system."

Women Suffer More Discrimination by the Judicial System than Men

Correctional Association of New York

The Correctional Association of New York is an independent, nonprofit organization that inspects New York prisons and reports its findings to the state legislature. In the following viewpoint, the association argues that the discrimination women often face in society is replicated in the criminal justice system. Using the New York prison system as an example, it points to the impact incarceration of women has on families, especially low-income and minority families. In addition, it asserts that imprisoned women are often victims of sexual abuse and mental illness and are given little access to programs that could help them overcome these challenges.

"Why Focus on Incarcerated Women?" Women in Prison Project, April 2009. Reproduced by permission of Correctional Association of New York. www.correctional association.org.

As you read, consider the following questions:

1. What percentage of women have given birth one year prior to or are pregnant at the time of their arrests?

2. What percentage of women are employed full time prior to their arrests?

3. What is the recidivism rate for women as compared to men?

Largely as a result of harsh, mandatory drug sentencing laws, the United States has witnessed an extraordinary increase in the number of incarcerated women. New York has been no exception: from 1973 to 2006, the number of women in New York State prisons increased by almost 645%. Almost 30,000 women are currently under custody of New York State or City criminal justice systems, either in prisons or jails, or on parole or probation. Along with the total prison population, the number of female inmates in New York has been steadily declining over the last nine years—in 2005, however, the female prison population rose by 1.7%. As of March 2006, there were 2,852 women in the state's correctional facilities.

Prison is an ineffective and inhumane response to the social ills that drive crime. The need to focus on women in prison does not deny the need to identify and address the difficulties that men prisoners face. However, because women have unique life experiences, occupy different familial and social roles, and commonly enter prison in more dire economic circumstances than men, criminal justice policies and programs must be created to suit women's particular needs and issues. Such a gender-specific approach would not only provide critical support for women in prison, but would also create a ripple effect of benefits for children, families and communities directly affected by incarceration.

The following is an explanation of some of these issues:

Women are more marginalized and discriminated against than men in all sectors of society; the unequal playing field that plagued an incarcerated woman before her arrest follows her through the criminal justice system. Failure to recognize and address the particular needs of women intensifies the difficulties they face at all points along the criminal justice continuum. Additionally, as women comprise a much smaller percentage of the total prison population than men, both in New York State (4.4%) and nationwide (7%), their specific problems are more easily overlooked.

The Impact on Families

Women's incarceration exacts a devastating social, emotional and economic toll on families and communities: about 75% of New York's female inmates reported being parents, compared to 58% of men. The majority of incarcerated mothers were the primary caretakers of their children, many as single parents. Women are also more likely than men to have more than one child. An estimated 11,000 children have a mother incarcerated in a New York prison or jail. Although over two-thirds come from—and will likely return to—New York City or its suburbs, more than 40% of New York's women prisoners are incarcerated in Albion Correctional Facility, located more than 370 miles away from their families and homes.

Most children with fathers incarcerated in New York live with their mothers, while most children of incarcerated mothers live with a grandparent, other relatives, or in foster care. Since New York enacted its own version of the federal Adoption and Safe Families Act (ASFA) in 1999, incarcerated mothers and fathers face an increased risk of permanently losing parental rights to their children. Under ASFA, if a child has been in foster care for 15 of the last 22 months, the foster care agency is almost always required to file a petition to terminate parental rights. The median minimum sentence for women in

New York State prisons—36 months—far exceeds this 15-month timeline, yet ASFA makes no exception for incarcerated parents. ASFA does have an exception for children placed in kinship care with relatives; because more children of incarcerated mothers are placed in foster care than children of incarcerated fathers, ASFA likely has a disproportionate affect on incarcerated mothers.

Nationally, 25% of adult women in prison either have given birth during the year prior to their incarceration or are pregnant at the time of their arrest. The New York State prison system has two nursery programs that allow incarcerated mothers to keep their infants with them for up to 18 months: one at Bedford Hills Correctional Facility, in New York's Westchester County, which has the capacity to house 26 mothers and infants, and another at Taconic Correctional Facility, also in Westchester County, which has the capacity to house 17 mothers and infants.

Women have lower incomes than men, less opportunity to make money, and a disproportionate responsibility for caring for their children and elderly relatives—labor that is often unpaid. Women commonly enter prison in more dire economic circumstances than men: nationally, about 40% of women prisoners were employed full-time prior to their arrest, compared with 60% of men; 37% of women prisoners had an income of less than $600 in the month prior to their arrest, compared with 28% of men; nearly 30% of women prisoners reported being on public assistance before arrest, compared to less than 8% of men. This harsh economic reality fuels women's illegal activity, like larceny, forgery, transporting or selling drugs, or prostitution.

Other Factors Affecting Women

Eight out of ten women who enter New York's criminal justice system each year are convicted of non-violent or "victimless" crimes; most women convicted of violent offenses have no

Conditions in Women's Prisons

Public financing for women's prisons is money misspent. There are alternatives to incarceration. Halfway houses and community-based programs that preserve family unity make more sense. They also operate at a far lower cost. Imprisoning parents tends to pass on a pattern of public institutionalization to the next generation. Children of imprisoned parents are five times more likely to become incarcerated themselves. Our children need us. Women need education, job training, abuse and drug counseling to help with parenting and childcare.

Sara Jane Olsen,
"The Conditions in Women's Prisons,"
Women and Prison: A Site for Resistance,
November 2007. www.womenandprison.org.

prior violent felony arrests or convictions. About 35% percent are incarcerated for drug offenses, compared with nearly 30% of men. Over 83% of women inmates in New York report having a substance abuse problem before their arrest, compared with 63% of male inmates. Nevertheless, alternative to incarceration programs specifically for women are few, and prison-based treatment opportunities are severely limited.

Women's incarceration, like men's, has a terrible and disproportionate effect on poor communities of color: more than 71% of New York's female inmates are African American or Latina, most of whom come from a handful of low-income urban neighborhoods in New York City. This statistic becomes even more skewed among women incarcerated for drug offenses: more than 82% are women of color.

An overwhelming majority of women inmates are survivors of physical or sexual abuse. A 1999 study of women incarcerated at Bedford Hills Correctional Facility found that more than 90% had endured sexual or physical violence in their lifetimes. Nationally, female inmates are up to eight times more likely than male inmates to report having been physically or sexually abused in their past. Women and girls who have experienced childhood violence are more likely to engage in criminalized self-destructive activities and be arrested than women whose lives are free from such trauma. Moreover, women inmates who have experienced violence are more likely than women without abuse histories to be targeted for sexual harassment and abuse from correction officers.

More than 14% of women in New York's prisons are known to be HIV+, a rate of infection almost double the rate for male inmates (7.3%), and more than 100 times the rate in the general public (.14%). About 23% of female inmates are infected with Hepatitis C (HCV), significantly higher than the rate of HCV infection for male inmates (13.6%).

Women inmates in New York suffer from mental illness at far higher rates than male inmates or women in the general public. The New York State Office of Mental Health has classified 30% of women under state custody as currently or potentially in need either of psychiatric treatment for a major mental disorder or of short-term therapy with medication, as compared to 11% of male inmates.

In New York State, almost 60% of women in prison have not finished high school; 40% read at an 8th grade level or below.

Lack of Programs and Services

Female inmates often do not have access to the same programs as male inmates. For example, New York State's Department of Correctional Services (DOCS) offers over 30 different vocational programs in male correctional facilities, and only 11 such programs at women's facilities. Over 30% of women in New York's prisons are currently on the waiting list for a vocational program. Another 11% have finished their vocational program assignment. Over 50% of the women at Albion are on the vocational program waiting list.

Like incarcerated men, women inmates commonly receive less than adequate services, including insufficient family reunification planning, substandard health care, and little opportunity for rehabilitation through substance abuse treatment, trauma counseling, and vocational and educational programs. These deficiencies undermine women's and men's ability to heal, take responsibility, and successfully reintegrate into their communities and reconnect with their families upon release.

Women are significantly less likely than men to recidivate: a recent DOCS study found that the three-year recidivism rate for women was approximately 28%, compared with a rate of 41% for men.

The stigma assigned to currently and formerly incarcerated women is often greater than the stigma assigned to their male counterparts. Women are generally stereotyped as more "passive" and less inclined to commit crimes than men. Female offenders are thus commonly considered to be even more "deviant" and "abnormal" than males who commit crimes.

| "Guard-on-prisoner sexual assault is a fact of life for many incarcerated women."

Women in Prison Are Sexually Vulnerable

Nicole Summer

Nicole Summer is a writer and lawyer based in New York City. In the following viewpoint, she argues that incarcerated women are being sexually assaulted in record numbers by prison guards. She asserts that rape is traumatic enough, but even more challenging for women in prison because they must face their attackers regularly and cannot easily report their crimes. The situation becomes even more complicated when pregnancy results from the sexual assault. Summer calls for more protection for female inmates and harsher punishments for guards who victimize them.

As you read, consider the following questions:

1. According to Sarah From, what percentage of women have been victims of sexual assault before being imprisoned?

Nicole Summer, "Powerless in Prison: Sexual Abuse Against Incarcerated Women," *RH Reality Check*, December 11, 2007. Reproduced by permission. This article was originally published at RH Reality Check, www.rhrealitycheck.org, an online daily publication covering global reproductive and sexual health and rights.

2. According to a 2004 Amnesty International report, what percentage of women are involved in sexual misconduct with prison guards?

3. Which two states pay for abortions for female prisoners who have suffered from sexual assault while incarcerated?

Surviving a sexual assault and then navigating the health care system to receive adequate counseling and reproductive medical attention is daunting enough for those who walk freely on the outside. For women in prison, these hurdles can seem insurmountable. Unfortunately, sexual assault, particularly guard-on-prisoner sexual assault, is a fact of life for many incarcerated women, and the ensuing implications for their reproductive health are many.

The power dynamics in prison severely disadvantage the prisoner, who is at the absolute mercy of her guards and correctional officers, relying on them for necessities such as food and for the small privileges and luxuries such as cigarettes. Guards have unlimited access to prisoners and their living environment, including where they sleep and where they bathe. With such an imbalance of power, the likelihood of sexual assault increases. Sexual abuse in prison can range from forcible rape to the trading of sex for certain privileges. While the latter may seem consensual to some, the drastic power disparity makes the idea of "consent" almost laughable. In fact, all 50 states have laws that make any sexual contact between inmates and correctional officers illegal, "consensual" or not. "It's *always* unacceptable and illegal," says Lovisa Stannow, executive director of Stop Prisoner Rape.

While guard-on-prisoner sexual assault is common, putting a number on the instances is difficult because so many assaults are unreported. As with sexual assault on the outside, many survivors in prison are ashamed and embarrassed to come forward, fear that their claim will be hard to prove or

fear that their attackers will retaliate. In prison the fear of retaliation is heightened, as the prisoner continues to live with
her attacker controlling her daily life. And inmates who report
a sexual assault are frequently put in segregated isolation, os-
tensibly to protect them from retaliation, but this isolation
can be emotionally and physically draining, and well, terribly
isolating. And many women in prison have been sexually
abused in the past, before they were incarcerated, or are ac-
customed to using sex to get what they want, on the inside or
the outside. "A lot of women don't view it as abuse," says
Deborah Golden, staff attorney at the D.C. Prisoners' Project
of the Washington Lawyers' Committee for Civil Rights and
Urban Affairs. About 80 percent of women inmates have already experienced some kind of sexual or physical abuse before prison, says Sarah From, director of public policy and
communications at the Women's Prison Association.

Despite the widespread underreporting, some statistics exist. First, there are about 200,000 women incarcerated in the
U.S. (in federal, state, local and immigration detention
settings), a number that is growing exponentially and that
makes up about 10 percent of the total prison population.
Amnesty International reports that in 2004, a total of 2,298
allegations of staff sexual misconduct against both male and
female inmates were made, and more than half of these cases
involved women as victims, a much higher percentage than
the 10 percent that women comprise of the total prison population. It can vary from institution to institution, but in the
worst prison facilities, one in four female inmates are sexually
abused in prison, says Stannow.

The Risk and Complications of Pregnancy

The risk of pregnancy as the result of a sexual assault is, of
course, a concern for many survivors, incarcerated or not. But
obtaining emergency contraception or an abortion, if one is
desired, may be more difficult for women on the inside. Be-

Sexual Abuse by Federal Prison Staff

Sexual abuse allegations against federal prison staff are reported to the Office of the Inspector General (OIG), the branch of the Justice Department that investigates such crimes. Here is a breakdown of nationwide cases from 2000 to 2004:

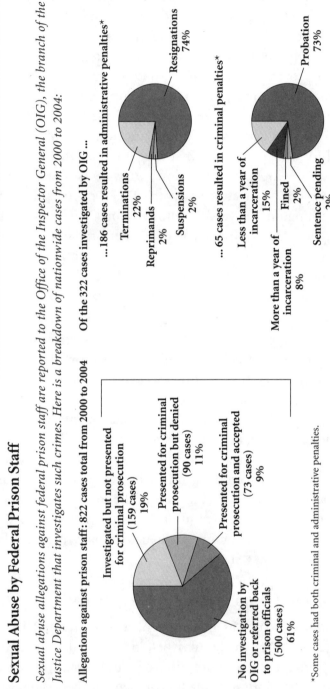

Allegations against prison staff: 822 cases total from 2000 to 2004

Investigated but not presented for criminal prosecution (159 cases) 19%

Presented for criminal prosecution but denied (90 cases) 11%

Presented for criminal prosecution and accepted (73 cases) 9%

No investigation by OIG or referred back to prison officials (500 cases) 61%

Of the 322 cases investigated by OIG ...

...186 cases resulted in administrative penalties*

Resignations 74%

Terminations 22%

Reprimands 2%

Suspensions 2%

...65 cases resulted in criminal penalties*

Probation 73%

Less than a year of incarceration 15%

More than a year of incarceration 8%

Fined 2%

Sentence pending 2%

*Some cases had both criminal and administrative penalties.

TAKEN FROM: Ruth Teichroeb, "Imprisoned, Unprotected," seattlepi.com, August 27, 2007.

cause many inmates do not report the sexual assault immediately (if at all), using emergency contraception is usually not possible, if it is even available. While prisoners' rights and reproductive rights organizations report hearing few complaints about emergency contraception being inaccessible to women in prison, they are unconvinced that it is widely available. Golden believes emergency contraception should be made readily available and should be on the prison's prescription formulary.

Unlike access to emergency contraception, access to abortion by inmates has seen its way through the courts. Crucially, women do not lose their right to decide to have an abortion just because they are in prison; rather, the issue is how the prison accommodates (or refuses to accommodate) her decision. "There are constitutional minimums," says Diana Kasdan, staff attorney with the ACLU's Reproductive Freedom Project. Although the details can vary from jurisdiction to jurisdiction, prisons must provide access to an abortion if one is desired. "Providing access" can range from providing transportation to an off-site medical facility, to allowing for a furlough or to providing abortions on-site, although Kasdan says she has not heard of the latter. A court in Arizona recently ruled that a court order to obtain transportation for an abortion cannot be required, and a federal court in Missouri ruled last year that a prison cannot refuse to pay for the transportation of inmates to receive abortions.

Paying for the abortion itself is yet another issue for women inmates, and it is a patchwork quilt of inconsistency throughout the states. Some state prison systems fund abortions, some states refuse to pay for what they consider "elective" abortions and some states simply have no official written policy, research by Rachel Roth has shown. Only two states specifically mention sexual assault in their prison abortion policies; both Minnesota and Wisconsin allow for government-subsidized abortions when the pregnancy results from a sexual assault. The federal Bureau of Prisons also pays for the abortion in the case of sexual assault.

In prison, the possibility of a coerced abortion can hang over an inmate who discovers she is pregnant as the result of a sexual assault by a guard. In a letter to Stop Prisoner Rape, one inmate writes:

> A rumor had spread through the facility that I was pregnant. I'm not sure how the rumor got started, but medical staff came to my cell and forced me to provide a urine sample that they could use to test for pregnancy. They did not ask me any questions, offer me any support, or seem at all concerned for my well-being. That same night, three guards, two female and one male, came into my cell, sprayed me in the face with mace, handcuffed me behind my back, threw me down on the ground, and said, "We hear you are pregnant by one of ours and we're gonna make sure you abort." The two female guards began to kick me as the male guard stood watch. The beating lasted about a minute, but it felt like ten or more. Afterwards, the male officer uncuffed me and they left.

The prisoner's rights as a mother, if she becomes pregnant and chooses not to terminate the pregnancy, are complicated, to say the least. Few jurisdictions allow women to keep their children in prison with them once they are born. Frequently, if there is no family member on the outside to take the child, the child will enter the foster care system, and the state will move to terminate the parental rights of the mother because she is absent. The parental rights of mothers in prison is a fraught and complicated issue, one that goes well beyond the particular problem of sexual assault by guards.

Help and Prevention

Access to counseling after a sexual assault in prison is virtually nonexistent. An inmate cannot simply call a hotline, since all calls are monitored and she has no privacy. When one inmate sought mental health care from prison services after a sexual assault, she was offered sleeping pills, says Golden. "There's no capacity in prisons for talk therapy," she says. And any counseling inside the prison is not confidential. Some community therapists will come in on visiting days to counsel an inmate, but usually only at the behest of a lawyer, says Golden.

Despite the overwhelming power imbalance, guard-on-prisoner sexual assault is preventable, insists Stannow. Efforts such as making sure the staff is well trained, educating the prisoners about their rights, eliminating impunity for guards and following up on reports of sexual abuse would go a long way toward prevention, she says. Congress had similar goals in mind when it unanimously passed the Prison Rape Elimination Act (PREA) in 2003. PREA aims to establish zero-tolerance standards of sexual assaults, to increase data and information on the occurrence of prison sexual assault and to develop and implement national standards for the detection, prevention, reduction and punishment of prison sexual assault. "PREA has been enormously important in ending sexual violence in detention," said Stannow. "Congress made clear that it's a problem that must be addressed." Perhaps most excitingly, PREA created a federal commission to generate binding national standards regarding sexual violence in detention. But "the existence of the law doesn't mean the problem is gone," Stannow continues. "Now we need to make sure that we build on the momentum of the law to make every corrections system in the country acknowledge that sexual violence in detention is a major problem, and does everything it can to end it."

One of the largest obstacles to eliminating prison sexual assault is the "social invisibility" of prisons. The general public neither knows nor cares about the plight of the incarcerated, and thus cannot demand that its government properly protect prisoners' bodily integrity and rights. Perhaps PREA is the beginning of the end of this social invisibility.

> "*Male rape victims may be even more likely than female victims to under-report out of intimidation or shame.*"

Men in Prison Are Sexually Vulnerable

Daniel Brook

Daniel Brook is a journalist and the author of The Trap: Selling Out to Stay Afloat in Winner-Take-All America. *In the following viewpoint, he argues that male prisoner rape remains a serious problem. He asserts that lack of protection by prison officials, poor facility construction, and apathy by the general public results in an acceptance of these violent acts. Although some local and state governments are working toward reducing prison rape, Brook claims that until societal attitudes about these crimes change, male inmates will continue to be sexually violated.*

As you read, consider the following questions:

1. According to the corrections industry, how many rapes occur in prisons each year?

2. How does San Francisco classify its prisoners upon admission?

Daniel Brook, "The Problem of Prison Rape," *Legal Affairs*, March/April 2004. Reproduced by permission. www.legalaffairs.org.

3. When did the U.S. government pass its first prison rape prevention legislation?

The prevalence of rape in prison *is* fearsome. Line officers recently surveyed in one southern state estimated that one in five male prisoners were being coerced into sex; among higher-ranking officials, the estimate was one in eight. Prisoners themselves estimated one in three. (Female prisoners are the victims of rape as well, though they are usually assaulted by male guards, not other inmates; the phenomenon of male-on-male prison rape is generally studied separately.)

Compiling statistics on prison rape involves the same pitfalls as compiling conventional rape statistics. Male rape victims may be even more likely than female victims to underreport out of intimidation or shame. Tom Cahill, whom I talked to at his home in Northern California, heads the board of directors of the advocacy group Stop Prisoner Rape; he was gang-raped in 1968 in a San Antonio jail where he was being held on a civil disobedience charge. "For males, it's the ultimate humiliation," he said. "And that silences most of us." Even without taking this reticence into account, the numbers are staggering. The most authoritative studies of the problem, conducted by the University of South Dakota professor Cindy Struckman-Johnson, found that over 20 percent of prisoners are the victims of some form of coerced sexual contact, and at least 7 percent are raped. Extrapolating from Struckman-Johnson's findings suggests that some 140,000 current inmates have been raped. The corrections industry itself estimates that there are 12,000 rapes per year, which exceeds the annual number of reported rapes in Los Angeles, Chicago, and New York combined.

Despite its prevalence, prison rape has generally been treated by courts and corrections officials as it has by novelists and filmmakers—as a problem without a solution. Prison rape is rarely prosecuted; like most crimes committed in prison, rapes aren't taken on by local district attorneys but left to corrections officials to handle. When inmates seek civil damages against the prison system . . . they must prove not merely that prison officials should have done more to prevent abuse but that they showed "deliberate indifference"—that is, that they had actual knowledge that an inmate was at risk and disregarded it. Showing that a prison guard should have known is not enough, no matter how obvious the signs of abuse.

This standard was established by the Supreme Court in the 1994 case *Farmer v. Brennan,* in which a transsexual inmate imprisoned for credit card fraud sued federal prison officials for ignoring his rape behind bars. While the court affirmed that prison rape is a violation of an inmate's constitutional rights and stated plainly that sexual assault is "not part of the penalty that criminal offenders pay for their offenses," it set up formidable barriers to establishing the culpability of corrections staff. At the cellblock level, the "deliberate indifference" standard discourages prison guards from shining a light into dark corners. What they don't know can't hurt them. . . .

Many people on the outside, including some within the criminal justice system, believe that prison rape is committed by "predatory homosexuals," a term used repeatedly in federal circuit court decisions. While inmate-on-inmate rape is in the most basic sense homosexual—both participants are male—researchers who have studied it have found that gay men are actually far more likely to be its victims than its perpetrators.

The feminist mantra that "rape isn't about sex, it's about power" may be even more applicable in the prison context, where it is common for men who would have never engaged in sexual contact with other men on the outside to become rapists when incarcerated. What's more, the relationship between rapist and victim in prison is often more than just a sexual one—it can devolve into out-and-out servitude. Victims are given women's names and made to perform household tasks such as cooking food, washing clothes, and cleaning the living space. . . .

The traditional rationale for prison rape is the lack of women, but most psychologists consider this facile. They see prison rape mainly as a means by which people who have been stripped of control over the most basic aspects of their lives—when to eat a meal, take a shower, or watch TV—can reclaim some sense of power. As one Louisiana prisoner, Wilbert Rideau, wrote, "the psychological pain involved in such an existence creates an urgent and terrible need for reinforcement of [a prisoner's] sense of manhood and personal worth." Others believe that prisoners become rapists out of fear of becoming victims themselves; it's a choice between becoming predator or prey. The psychologist Daniel Lockwood, in his study *Prison Sexual Violence*, calls this strategy "pre-emptive self-defense."

County Jail No. 3 sits on a landscaped hill in San Bruno, [California], and when the sun shines on its Art Deco façade, you can see what a proud accomplishment it must have been for California law enforcement back in the *Dragnet* [a popular TV crime drama from the 1950s and 1960s set in Los Angeles] era. On the inside, however, the prison is crumbling. I traveled to the prison's fourth floor in its manually operated elevator, a harrowing experience I shared with Eileen Hirst, the chief of staff for the San Francisco County sheriff, and with a sheriff's deputy who trailed along to ensure our safety.

When we arrived at the night guard's post, Hirst issued a polite order. "Stand here," she said, putting me in the spot where the guard would keep watch. "Can you see anything that's going on in any cell?" Looking down the narrow whitewashed corridor, I couldn't even say for sure that there were cells in this cellblock, and I certainly couldn't see any of the prisoners sitting inside them. Anything could have been happening behind the bars.

Hirst was willing to show off this obvious rape trap because a 1994 federal court decision had ordered that the out-of-date facility be closed. County Jail No. 3 will be decommissioned by the end of the year [2004], replaced by a new, state-of-the-art facility. The changes were brought about by *Besk v. City and County of San Francisco*, a case that originated with an allegation of prison rape and eventually turned into a broader class-action suit about overcrowding. In its decision, a federal court mandated that the county build new state-of-the-art prisons, essentially ordering the San Francisco Board of Supervisors to come up with the necessary funds.

Reducing Prison Rape

Even before *Besk*, however, San Francisco County had been a leader in trying to reduce sexual assaults in prison. In part thanks to its large and vocal gay community, San Francisco was one of the first jurisdictions to start asking about the sexual orientation of newly arrived inmates. In 1979, Michael Hennessey, a young lawyer, was elected sheriff of San Francisco, a position he still holds. A campaign poster from Hunter S. Thompson's run for sheriff of Aspen, [Colorado], hangs in Hennessey's office, an acknowledgement, perhaps, that only in San Francisco could a prisoners' rights advocate be put in charge of the county jail system.

Hennessey's 1979 campaign manager, who was gay, made him aware of the problem of prison rape. Hennessey promised to create a classification system that would house gay men separately in the county's jails. After he was elected, Hennessey says, "gay men were housed together in a gay tank, or what they called a 'queens' tank.'"

The current classification system is more sophisticated. After new inmates are booked, they're interviewed, sometimes for as long as 45 minutes. Inmates are sorted into three classification levels—minimum, medium, and maximum—based on their likelihood of harming fellow inmates. The levels do not correspond to the crimes these people committed but to the amount of jail time they have under their belt.

Characteristics of Male Prison Rape Victims

Specifically, prisoners fitting any part of the following description are more likely to be targeted: young, small in size, physically weak, white, gay, first offender, possessing "feminine" characteristics such as long hair or a high voice; being unassertive, unaggressive, shy, intellectual, not street-smart, or "passive"; or having been convicted of a sexual offense against a minor. Prisoners with any one of these characteristics typically face an increased risk of sexual abuse, while prisoners with several overlapping characteristics are much more likely than other prisoners to be targeted for abuse.

The characteristics of prison rapists are somewhat less clear and predictable, but certain patterns can nonetheless be discerned. First, although some older inmates commit rape, the perpetrators also tend to be young, if not always as young as their victims—generally well under thirty-five years old. They are frequently larger or stronger than their victims, and are generally more assertive, physically aggressive, and more at home in the prison environment. They are "street smart"—often gang members. They have typically been convicted of more violent crimes than their victims.

Human Rights Watch,
"Predators and Victims," No Escape:
Male Rape in U.S. Prisons, *2001. www.hrw.org.*

San Francisco's first attempt at a classification system separated gays from straights and violent offenders from nonviolent offenders, but Hennessey has found that sorting prisoners by their vulnerability is more effective. "You might be charged with murder because you murdered your spouse or your parent or your child, but you've never been in jail before in your life. You're a vulnerable person, you're not a really tough guy," he said. On the other hand, another inmate "might be in for drunk driving, but might have just gotten out of San Quentin last week. So you can't just go by their charge. You have to go by their background and by their criminal sophistication."

San Francisco's classification system has not eliminated rapes in the county's jails, but the city has found ways to drastically reduce the rate of sexual assault in a corrections facility. The efforts have also demonstrated, however, that such reforms do not come cheap. Despite Hennessey's desire to address the rape problem, it took the *Besk* case to get the funding to build new jails. Hennessey, a named defendant in the case, said he was more than happy to comply with the court's order to build new facilities. "Jails and prisons do not have many friends," he said. "Spending money on them is not a big vote-getter." Only half-joking, he said, "it's wonderful to be sued."

County Jail No. 8, which sits on a city block in San Francisco's South of Market neighborhood once home to dot-com start-ups, is one of the new jails built with money from *Besk*. Eileen Hirst and I stood at the elevated guard station in one of the pods. The station, decked out with controls, monitors, and a swivel chair, felt a bit like the bridge of the Starship Enterprise. With the cells arrayed in a semicircle, from the guard's chair I could see into each cell, just as an actor on an amphitheater stage can make eye contact with every audience member. Instead of bars, the cell doors had large glass windows. Overcrowding remains a problem, and some inmates in County Jail No. 8 are double-celled. But according to Lt. Sonny Bruno, who is in charge of classification at the new jail, overcrowding has not yet led to rape. "I don't have knowledge of anyone who's reported a sex assault in these pods," she said.

Challenging Views on Prison Rape

In 1826, in what was likely the first published mention of prison rape in the history of the republic, the Rev. Louis Dwight wrote that "Boys are Prostituted to the Lust of old Convicts" throughout the institutions he surveyed from Massachusetts to Georgia. Dwight, the founder of the Prison Discipline Society of Boston, a prison reform group, wrote that "Nature and humanity cry aloud for redemption from this dreadful degradation." It was not until the 21st century, however, that the nation saw its first anti-prison-rape legislation.

Last year [2003], Congress passed the Prison Rape Reduction Act, which allocates $60 million to support rape-prevention programs run by federal, state, and local corrections staff and to aid investigations and punishment of perpetrators. The bill, which enjoyed bipartisan support in the House and the Senate, also requires states to collect statistics on prison rape. Backers of the legislation hope federal oversight will make sexual assault prevention a priority for jail and prison systems across the nation. But $60 million can only go so far. The facility that will replace County Jail No. 3 in San Francisco, slated to open by year's end [2004] cost nearly twice that amount.

Congress's money will certainly make some difference, and more might be allocated in the future. A higher hurdle, however, is the task of changing the way Americans think about prison rape. . . .

In *Butler v. Dowd*, a Missouri jury found that three inmates had been raped due to deliberate indifference from the staff, violating the inmates' Eighth Amendment right to be free of "cruel and unusual" punishment. In another case in Connecticut, *James v. Tilghman*, a jury found that corrections officials' decision to place an inmate in a cell with a suspected sexual predator similarly violated the prisoner's constitutional rights. In those cases, the juries awarded the inmates $1 and nothing, respectively. Both "awards" were upheld on appeal.

"Race is often the decisive factor in guiding law enforcement decisions about who to stop, search, or question."

Minorities Are Unfairly Targeted by Law Enforcement

Leadership Conference on Civil Rights Education Fund

The Leadership Conference on Civil Rights Education Fund (LCCREF) is the education and research division of the Civil Rights Coalition and works toward securing equal opportunities for all Americans. In the following viewpoint, the LCCREF argues that racial profiling, or the unfair targeting of minorities by law enforcement, remains a significant problem in the United States. Although the focus of such profiling has shifted over the years, the practice continues to affect thousands of minorities in many situations, including while driving, walking, and even traveling by air.

As you read, consider the following questions:

1. How does the author define racial profiling?

2. What is "driving while black"?

3. According to a 1999 report by the New York State Attorney General, what percentage of motorists stopped by NYPD police officers were black or Hispanic?

In May 1992, Robert Wilkins, a Harvard-trained African American attorney, was returning home from a family funeral in Chicago with three members of his extended family, two males and one female. While driving in a rental vehicle on the interstate highway near Cumberland, Maryland, they were pulled over for speeding by a state trooper who asked for consent to search the vehicle. Wilkins, fully aware of his constitutional rights, refused to consent to a search. The officer detained Wilkins and his family outside the car for almost an hour, in the rain, until a drug-sniffing dog was brought to search the vehicle. The search turned up nothing and the police officer simply issued a ticket. Wilkins later learned that his family had been stopped because he and his relatives fit the profile developed and used by Maryland State Police to uncover drug-running activity along the highway: they were male, Black, and driving a rental car.

In October 1999, Alberto Lovato, a 29-year-old Latino musician, was pulled over by a Los Angeles police officer, allegedly for using the right turn lane to pass other vehicles. Police records show that the officer stopped Mr. Lovato more than 15 miles away from the site of the alleged violation. The officer did not ask for Mr. Lovato's license or registration; instead he drew his gun and told Mr. Lovato to get out of his car and lie face down on the ground. After two other officers arrived, Mr. Lovato was frisked, handcuffed so tightly that he sustained serious cuts on his wrists, and detained for more than an hour while he was questioned about gang membership, drugs and weapons. Eventually the officers took Mr. Lovato to jail where he was detained for several more hours.

In 1993, two 15-year old Asian American girls, Minhtran Tran and Quyen Pham, were shopping in a strip mall in Garden Grove, California. Both girls were honor students and had never had any contact with law enforcement. As they were leaving the mall, the girls were confronted by Garden Grove police who accused them of making trouble and asked whether the girls belonged to gangs. The police questioned the girls, placed them against a wall and, without their consent, photographed them. Although the girls had not been charged or cited and had done nothing wrong, their photograph was posted in the Garden Grove Police Department. The police maintained that the girls had been identified as wrongdoers because they were dressed in "gang attire." In fact, the girls were dressed in form fitting shirts and baggy pants—common dress for American teenagers. What soon became evident was that the girls' race determined their treatment by the police: Orange County police had specifically identified Asian youth as being involved in gang activity.

On September 14, 2001, an Indian American motorist and three family members were pulled over and ticketed by a Maryland state trooper because their car had broken taillights. The trooper interrogated the family, questioned them about their nationality, and asked for proof of citizenship. When the motorist said that their passports were at home, the officer allegedly stated, "You are lying. You are Arabs involved in terrorism." He ordered them out of the car, had them put their hands on the hood, and searched the car. When he discovered a knife in a toolbox, the officer handcuffed the driver and later reported that the driver "wore and carried a butcher knife, a dangerous deadly weapon, concealed upon and about his person." The driver was detained for several hours but eventually released.

Understanding Racial Profiling

The individuals described above were all investigated by police who considered race in determining who should be suspected of criminal activity. Certain minorities, the officers assumed, are more likely than other people to engage in certain types of criminal behavior. When it came time for these police officers to exercise discretion about who to stop for conduct that thousands of Americans engage in—i.e., committing minor traffic violations or dressing a certain way—these officials chose to stop and detain minorities. The police engaged in this activity without any actual evidence, such as a suspect description, that any of the individuals stopped had committed a crime. In all these cases, race became a proxy for specific evidence of involvement in criminal activity. This is the essence of racial profiling.

Racial profiling is *any* use of race, religion, ethnicity, or national origin by law enforcement agents as a means of deciding who should be investigated, *except* where these characteristics are part of a specific suspect description. Under this definition, racial profiling doesn't only occur when race is the *sole* criterion used by a law enforcement agent in determining who to investigate. Such a definition would be far too narrow. Several of the individuals described above were accused of committing traffic violations, and the Supreme Court has held that the law enforcement practice of stopping vehicles for traffic violations as a pretext for investigating more serious crimes is constitutional. Ms. Tran and Ms. Pham were suspected of gang activity because they were allegedly wearing "gang attire." Indeed, most law enforcement criminal profiles refer to race as one of many factors to guide law enforcement discretion.

Today, overt racism is roundly condemned whenever it comes to light, and it is rare for individuals to be targeted by law enforcement agents *solely* because of their race. However, as demonstrated by the above examples and by the raft of empirical evidence developed in recent years (discussed below), race is often the *decisive* factor in guiding law enforcement decisions about who to stop, search, or question. Selective enforcement based in part on race is no less pernicious or offensive to the principle of equal justice than is enforcement based solely on race. Indeed, because the former form of selective

People of Color Are Disproportionately Targeted by Police

- Among persons over age 24, Blacks (11.2%) were significantly more likely to be pulled over while driving than Whites (8.9%).

- Among drivers stopped for speeding, Blacks (75.7%) and Hispanics (79.4%) were more likely than Whites (66.6%) to be ticketed.

- Police were more likely to conduct a search of the vehicle and/or driver in traffic stops involving Black male drivers (15.9%) or Hispanic male drivers (14.2%), compared to White male drivers (7.9%).

- Blacks (5.2%) and Hispanics (4.2%) stopped by police while driving are more likely than Whites (2.6%) to be arrested.

- In other words, Blacks composed 11.6% of drivers stopped by police, but represented 19.9% of the drivers arrested. Hispanics were 8.4% of drivers stopped by police, but 11.7% of those arrested. Whites, on the other hand, are 77% of stopped drivers but only 66.3% of drivers arrested.

Political Research Associates,
"How Is the Criminal Justice System Racist?"
Defending Justice: An Activist Resource Kit, *May 2005.*
www.publiceye.org.

enforcement is more prevalent and more subtle than explicit racism, it may be more damaging to our criminal justice system and constitutional fabric.

"Driving While Black or Brown"

The practice of racial profiling can take many forms, the most notorious of which is the "driving while Black" phenomenon illustrated by the Robert Wilkins case. In this scenario, law enforcement agents use selective enforcement of traffic laws as a pretext for stopping and searching Black motorists, who, according to the law enforcement rationale, are particularly likely to be engaged in illegal drug activity. As Alberto Lovato's story demonstrates, Hispanic motorists have also drawn unwarranted attention from the police ("driving while brown"). This is especially true in border areas where enforcement of the drug laws dovetails with enforcement of the immigration laws. And, as demonstrated by the account of the Indian American motorist described above, Arabs, Muslims, Sikhs, and South Asians have increasingly come under suspicion for "driving while Arab" since [the terrorist attacks of] September 11 [2001].

For decades, the "driving while Black or brown" phenomenon was well known in the minority population, but largely unnoticed among other Americans. But beginning in the 1990s, empirical evidence emerged to support the anecdotal accounts of racial profiling on America's highways. This evidence demonstrated that Black and other minority motorists were and are being stopped at a rate far out of proportion to their presence in the overall population or on the highways. For example

- A U.S. Department of Justice report on police contacts with the public concluded that in 1999, African Americans were 20 percent more likely to be stopped than White Americans, and 50 percent more likely than Whites to have experienced more than one stop. Police were more than twice as likely to search an African American or Hispanic driver than a White driver.

- In the three-year period from January 1995 to December 1997, Blacks comprised more than 70 percent of the drivers stopped and searched by the Maryland State Highway Patrol, although they made up only 17.5 percent of the overall drivers (and overall speeders). These disparities were explained by a state document called the "Criminal Intelligence Report," which contained an explicit policy targeting Black motorists.

- A study of traffic stops on the New Jersey Turnpike between 1988–1991 found that Blacks were 35 percent of those stopped, though only 13.5 percent of the cars on the turnpike had a Black occupant and Blacks were only 15 percent of all traffic violators. A 1999 State Attorney General's Report studying Turnpike stops and searches in 1997–1998 concluded that almost 80 percent of searches involved Blacks and other minorities.

- In the early 1990s, an investigation of the practices of the Volusia County, Florida Sheriff's Department revealed that although Blacks or Hispanics were only 5 percent of the drivers on a portion of I-95 that ran through the county, they were nearly 70 percent of drivers stopped on that stretch of highway. Blacks and Hispanics were not only stopped more than Whites, they were also stopped for longer periods of time than Whites.

Recent studies confirm the persistence of the "driving while Black or brown" phenomenon. LAPD data for the period July–November 2002 reveals that while Blacks comprised only 10 percent of the overall population of Los Angeles, they were 18 percent of those subjected to traffic stops. Moreover, 22 percent of Blacks who were stopped were asked to step out of their cars, as compared to only 7 percent of Whites stopped. Once out of their cars, 67 percent of Blacks were patted down and 85 percent subjected to a body search. Fifty-five percent of Hispanics removed from their cars were patted down and 84 percent searched. By contrast, only 50 percent of Whites were patted down and 71 percent searched. . . .

"Stop and Frisk" Tactics

Just as minority *motorists* are subject to profiling, so too are minority *pedestrians*. This is especially true with the advent of community-based policing strategies, which often provide street level law enforcement officers with wide discretion to "clean up" the communities they patrol by whatever means seem expedient. As Professor Angela Davis has noted, "The practical effect of this deference [to law enforcement discretion] is the assimilation of police officers' subjective beliefs, biases, hunches, and prejudices into law." And, as in the motor vehicle context, such discretion in the pedestrian context is exercised to the detriment of minorities, who are perceived to pose a threat to public safety even if they have done nothing wrong. African American Harvard Law Professor Charles Ogletree says, "If I'm dressed in a knit cap and hooded jacket, I'm probable cause."

The "stop and frisk" practices of the New York City Police Department in the 1990s demonstrate how community policing can turn into racial profiling. Predictably, Black and Hispanic New Yorkers were disproportionately targeted for stop and frisk patdowns. A December 1999 report by the New York State Attorney General found that of the 175,000 stops engaged in by NYPD officers from January 1988 through March 1999, almost 84 percent were of Blacks and Hispanics, despite the fact that those groups made up less than half of New York City's population. By contrast, only 13 percent of the stops were of White New Yorkers, who make up 43 percent of the city's population. The state Attorney General also identified racial disparities in stop rates within White neighborhoods—in precincts that were approximately 90 percent White, more than 53 percent of the total stops were of Blacks and Hispanics. Thus, more stops of minorities occurred in general in the city, and more stops of minorities than of Whites occurred even in majority-White neighborhoods.

Recent pedestrian stop statistics from Los Angeles are consistent with those from New York City. While Blacks make up only 11 percent of the population of Los Angeles, they were subjected to 36 percent of the pedestrian stops. Meanwhile Whites, who make up 30 percent of the city's population, were subjected to only 18 percent of the stops. Only 24 percent of Whites who were stopped in Los Angeles were searched, while nearly half of Blacks and Hispanics stopped were searched. Overall, Whites were 11 percent of those searched, Blacks 40 percent, and Hispanics 46 percent.

Racial profiling of pedestrians in New York has contributed to several well-publicized tragedies in recent years. Amadou Diallo was a young Black man living in a predominantly minority neighborhood in New York City. On the night of February 4, 1999, Diallo was approached by four NYPD officers as he stood by the front steps of his apartment building. He reached for his wallet to produce identification, and the police officers, thinking that Diallo was reaching for a gun, fired 41 gunshots and killed him. Testifying in his own defense, one of the officers who shot Diallo noted that "[t]he way he was peering up and down the block" had made the officers suspicious. "He stepped backward, back into the vestibule as we were approaching, like he didn't want to be seen . . . and I'm trying to figure out what's going on. You know— what's this guy up to? I was getting a little leery, from the training, of my past experience of arrests, involving gun arrests." It is hard to imagine that Diallo's race did not contribute to the officers' unwarranted suspicions.

The same assumptions that lead police to engage in disproportionate stops of minority drivers leads them to engage in disproportionate stops of minority pedestrians. For Amadou Diallo and others like him, these assumptions produced tragic results. The Diallo case made headlines throughout the country, but countless incidents that do not result in death occur every day and escape public notice. These incidents contribute to a well-grounded fear among minorities that the police will assume the worst about them, and on a dark street corner that assumption can be fatal.

Customs Service Profiling

Racial profiling at U.S. ports of entry has long been commonplace. Drug courier profiles used by the Customs Service have regularly included race as a factor in guiding law enforcement discretion. Anecdotal and, later, statistical evidence revealed that the Customs Service was disproportionately targeting Black women as part of its drug interdiction efforts, based on the assumption that Black women were likely to act as couriers of drugs into the United States.

The experience of Yvette Bradley is illustrative. On April 5, 1999, Ms. Bradley, an advertising executive, returned to the United States from a vacation to Jamaica with her sister. While going through customs at Newark International Airport, Ms. Bradley and her sister were both drawn aside for searches of their luggage—searches which, they noticed, were being carried out on large numbers of Black female passengers, but few White females. After her luggage had been searched, Ms. Bradley was directed to a room off to the side of the customs clearance area. In that room, Ms. Bradley was subjected to a humiliating body search, which included a (female) Customs agent touching her breasts and genital area and actually penetrating her. The search turned up nothing.

A 2000 General Accounting Office Report on U.S. Customs Service practices confirmed Ms. Bradley's perception that Black females were being targeted for searches by Customs officials. Data from 102,000 personal searches conducted by the Customs Service in 1997–1998 revealed that in Fiscal Year 1998, Black female U.S. citizens were nine times more likely, and Hispanic female U.S. citizens four times more likely, than White female U.S. citizens to be x-rayed on suspicion of drug smuggling. Black women were also more likely than any other groups to be strip-searched. Black and Hispanic men and women were more likely overall to be x-rayed after being patted down or frisked than White men and women.

"High black arrest rates appear to reflect high crime rates, not police misconduct."

Minorities Are Not Unfairly Targeted by Law Enforcement

New Century Foundation

The New Century Foundation is a nonprofit organization founded in 1994 to study immigrant and race relations in the United States. In the following viewpoint, the foundation argues that blacks and other minorities are not unfairly targeted by law enforcement. In fact, according to its data, blacks are far more likely to commit crimes than any other racial group. The organization asserts that police officers would have nothing to gain by arresting innocent African Americans, especially given the potential for scandal erupting over false arrests.

As you read, consider the following questions:

1. What four things must happen for a person to go to jail?

2. According to the Uniform Crime Reports (UCR), what percentage of arrests in 2002 were of black criminals?

The Color of Crime: Race, Crime, and Justice in America. Oakton, VA: New Century Foundation, 2005. Copyright © 2005 New Century Foundation. Reproduced by permission of American Renaissance. www.colorofcrime.com.

3. What percentage of blacks who were reported to the police were likely to be arrested as compared to people of other races who committed the same crimes?

In March 11, 2005, Brian Nichols, who was on trial for rape, went on a murderous rampage at an Atlanta courthouse, shooting a judge, a court reporter, and a deputy. After his arrest, he explained that he was a "soldier on a mission" against a racially biased legal system. In jail awaiting his rape trial, he had been angry to find so many other black inmates, and he wondered how many were innocent. For him, the large number of blacks meant the legal system was "systematic slavery."

Mr. Nichols's views were only an extreme version of what a majority of black Americans believe. A 2003 national poll found that only 28 percent of blacks, as opposed to 66 percent of whites, thought whites and blacks receive equal treatment at the hands of the police.

This widely-held view that the police are biased is not supported by the evidence. The data suggest the criminal justice system generally treats offenders of different races equally. High arrest and incarceration rates for blacks and Hispanics—and very low rates for Asians—reflect differences in crime rates, not police or justice system bias.

Many Americans also have misconceptions about interracial crime, believing that whites are the primary perpetrators. In fact, blacks are far more likely to commit crimes against whites than vice versa.

It is also common to assume that if different groups commit crimes at different rates, it is because of poverty and other forms of social disadvantage. This is a plausible argument, but controlling for social disparities does not greatly reduce race differences in crime rates. This suggests differences would remain even if the races were economically and socially equal.

Most Americans at least suspect that blacks and Hispanics are more likely to commit crimes than whites or Asians. The data supports this view. However, the crime statistics published by the federal government and reported in the press are incomplete and often confusing. It takes real digging to get a clear picture of racial differences in crime rates—and they can be great. . . .

Government reports usually treat blacks clearly and consistently, so they are the group about which we have the best information. They are also the group generally thought to be the worst victims of justice system bias, so we will concentrate on blacks in searching for bias.

Are Police Biased?

For someone to go to prison, four things have to happen. The police must arrest him for a felony, charges must be filed, he must plead or be found guilty, and a judge must sentence him to prison. Racial bias could enter at any stage.

Blacks are certainly more likely to be arrested than other groups. According to the Uniform Crime Reports (UCR), blacks accounted for 27 percent of arrests in 2002, even though they were only 13 percent of the population, whereas whites and Hispanics (W&H) accounted for 71 percent of arrests, but were 81 percent of the population. This means that when all crime categories are added together, blacks were more than twice as likely to be arrested as W&H. Blacks were four times more likely to be arrested for violent crimes, and no fewer than eight times more likely to be arrested for robbery.

Many people believe blacks are arrested so often because police target them unfairly. Brian Nichols, the Atlanta gunman, seems to think police are arresting blacks *en masse* whether they are guilty or not. Many local authorities have passed laws to correct what they believe to be police bias. Police argue that they are targeting criminals, not non-whites, and that they arrest large numbers of minorities only because minorities are committing a large number of crimes.

The best test of police bias is to compare an independent and objective count of the percentage of criminals who are black with the percentage of arrested suspects who are black. If they are about the same—if, for example, we can determine that half the robbers are black, and we find that about half the robbers the police arrest are black—it is good evidence police are not targeting blacks unfairly.

But what information do we have about the race of criminals other than arrest reports? The best independent source is the National Crime Victimization Survey (NCVS). For the most recent report, the government surveyed 149,040 people about crimes of which they had been victims during 2003. They described the crimes in detail, including the race of the perpetrator, and whether they reported the crimes to the police. The survey sample, which is massive by polling standards, was carefully chosen to be representative of the entire US population. By comparing information about races of perpetrators with racial percentages in arrest data from the Uniform Crime Reports (UCR) we can determine if the proportion of criminals the police arrest who are black is equivalent to the proportion of criminals the victims say were black.

UCR and NCVS reports for the years 2001 through 2003 offered the most recent data on crimes suffered by victims, and arrests for those crimes. Needless to say, many crimes are not reported to the police, and the number of arrests the police make is smaller still. An extrapolation from NCVS data gives a good approximation of the actual number of crimes committed in the United States every year. The NCVS tells us that between 2001 and 2003, there were an estimated 1.8 million robberies, for example, of which 1.1 million were reported to the police. The UCR tell us that in the same period police made 229,000 arrests for robbery. Police cannot make an arrest if no one tells them about a crime, so the best way to see if police are biased is to compare the share of offenders who are black in crimes reported to the police, and the share of those arrested who are black. . . .

For most crimes, police are arresting fewer blacks than would be expected from the percentage of criminals the victims tell us are black (rape/sexual assault is the only exception). In the most extreme case, burglary, victims tell police that 45 percent of the perpetrators were black, but only 28 percent of the people arrested for that crime were black. If all the NCVS crimes are taken together, blacks who committed crimes that were reported to the police were 26 percent less likely to be arrested than people of other races who committed the same crimes.

These figures lend no support to the charge that police arrest innocent blacks, or at least pursue them with excessive zeal. In fact, they suggest the opposite, that police are more determined to arrest non-black rather than black criminals. . . .

Although blacks are 13 percent of the population, they commit a far larger percentage of every crime included in the NCVS. They are eight times more likely than people of other races to rob someone, for example, and 5.5 times more likely to steal a car. . . .

Practicalities of Police Bias

The more seriously one thinks about arrest bias, the less likely it seems. How does it work? Do police deliberately arrest innocent blacks and Hispanics but ignore white and Asian criminals? If the victim of a crime says he was attacked by a white man, police cannot very well go out and arrest a black. Or do they simply make no effort to find white or Asian criminals? If DNA from a crime scene turns out to be from a white person, do police stop trying to solve the case? If police see a white or Asian breaking into a building do they ignore him? Or, at the same time, do police try to clear crimes by arresting people—presumably blacks—they know are probably innocent? None of this makes sense. Police officers win recognition and advancement for making arrests, but only if arrests lead to convictions. The justice system does not reward false arrests or lackadaisical law enforcement.

Likewise, every officer in the country knows that race is potentially explosive. Every officer knows minority communities—blacks, especially—publicize and demonstrate against what they see as bias. Police know they are under scrutiny from activist organizations and city governments, and that officers lose jobs over race scandals. It would take a very determined racist to risk his job in order to indulge prejudice.

The fear of scandal may even explain why arrest rates for blacks are lower than their offense rates. In uncertain cases, officers may let a black suspect go rather than risk a scandal. Under the same circumstances they might arrest a white because there will be no scandal. As a practical matter, it is not easy to see how police can work systematic racial bias into their jobs.

Or is it? When it comes to what are called discretionary arrests, police actually can vent prejudices if they want. When there is a murder or a rape, police are under pressure to catch the criminal. It is not a matter of making an arrest—or not—only if they feel like it. The police have much more leeway with crimes like public drunkenness or disorderly conduct. They can drive right past a drunk and do nothing, or they can stop and arrest him, so crimes of this kind, in which police have a choice about whether they take action, are the perfect opportunity for bias.

If officers are prejudiced, therefore, one would expect blacks to figure in even greater disproportions in discretionary arrests than they do in serious crimes. They do not. Racial differences in arrest rates for drunkenness, disorderly conduct, drunk driving and vagrancy, and other offenses in which arrest is discretionary are smaller than for violent crimes. The 2002 UCR show blacks and W&H were equally likely to be arrested for drunkenness, for example, but blacks were 6.6 times more likely to be arrested for murder.

It is clear, therefore, that the only evidence for police bias is disproportionate arrest rates for those groups police critics say are the targets of bias. High black arrest rates appear to reflect high crime rates, not police misconduct. . . .

Blacks Are More Likely to Commit Crimes

This report takes no position on causes of group differences in crime rates, except to point out that the ones that are most commonly proposed—poverty, unemployment, lack of education—are not satisfactory. As for the reality of those differences, the evidence is overwhelming: Blacks are considerably more likely than any other group to commit crimes of virtually all kinds, while Asians are least likely. Whites and Hispanics have intermediate crime rates. There can be debate about the exact extent of the differences—the data do not make these calculations easy—but differences are a fact.

These differences are far greater than some that have given rise to significant public initiatives. Blacks are more than twice as likely as whites to be unemployed, and white household income is 60 percent higher than black household income. Blacks are twice as likely as whites to drop out of high school. Race differences of this kind have led to everything from affirmative action preferences to No Child Left Behind legislation.

Americans are right to be concerned about these differences, but they are, relatively speaking, small. To repeat some of the more substantial differences in crime rates: Blacks are about eight times more likely than whites to commit murder, and *25 times* more likely than Asians to do so. Blacks are 15 times more likely than whites to go to prison for robbery, and *50 times* more likely than Asians. Crime reduction programs analogous to No Child Left Behind may or may not be practical, but no solutions will be found if we avert our eyes from these differences.

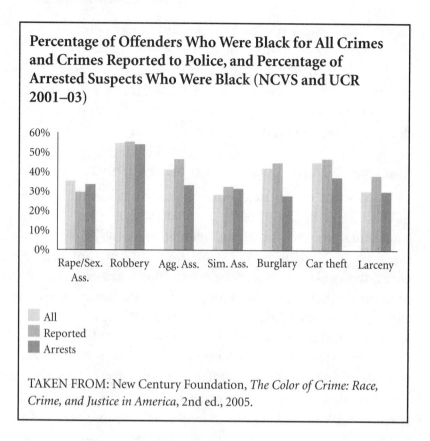

Percentage of Offenders Who Were Black for All Crimes and Crimes Reported to Police, and Percentage of Arrested Suspects Who Were Black (NCVS and UCR 2001–03)

TAKEN FROM: New Century Foundation, *The Color of Crime: Race, Crime, and Justice in America*, 2nd ed., 2005.

The Dangers of Misunderstandings

A better understanding of the facts is important for other reasons. The evidence suggests that deeply-rooted assumptions about police bias are wrong. Many Americans believe that entire professions—police, prosecutors, judges—are systematically biased against minorities (critics usually have nothing to say about low incarceration rates for Asians, but if they were consistent they would argue that the police and the courts must be biased in favor of Asians). This is insulting and unfair. Not only does it reflect abiding prejudice against some of the most hard-working people in America, it leads to onerous anti-"racial profiling" regulations that require police to fill in detailed racial information about every traffic stop, stop-and-frisk, or search. Additional paperwork is a distraction from the job that really matters: stopping crime.

Assumptions about police bias are especially common among minority groups that have the most to gain from good relations with the police. Blacks, in particular, are convinced of police "racism." In extreme cases, this belief leads to murderous rampages like that of Brian Nichols with which this report begins. It is not an exaggeration to say that his victims might be alive today if the facts in this report were widely known. In countless less severe cases, a belief in police bias leads to suspicion, resentment, and lack of cooperation, all of which make it harder for the police to do their jobs, and more likely that minorities will suffer from crimes that could have been solved or prevented. How often do assumptions about police—and societal—racism so anger blacks that they go beyond lack of cooperation to crime itself? It is profoundly destructive for minorities to have exaggerated resentments toward the society in which they live. Uncritical repetition by whites of assertions about police bias only deepens these resentments.

A proper understanding of crime rates also supports a common-sense understanding of race and is an antidote to hypocrisy. Americans do not know the exact statistics, but they know that whites (and Asians) are less likely than blacks to rob them. Even many people who insist that black arrest rates are bloated by police bias are careful to avoid certain neighborhoods. Group differences as great as those in this report are a reality that filters into public awareness even if the press seldom reports them.

It is common to oppose publication of crime statistics for fear of creating "negative stereotypes," but statistical differences are the basis for important policy decisions. If one airline were three times more likely than other airlines to be involved in fatal accidents, would it be reasonable to avoid it? If one brand of decongestant were twice as likely as another to have serious side effects, would the FDA be justified in investigating it? Many people pay for optional side airbags in automobiles. Does this cut the risk of death or injury in half? More than that? Less? People make choices, and risk affects their choices. If there are different risks associated with different groups of people it is legitimate to investigate and weigh those risks.

Finally, immigration is rapidly changing the population of the United States. Thanks to immigration, Hispanics are now the nation's largest minority group. Hispanics are one of the more crime-prone groups in America. They also have high rates of illegitimacy, school failure, poverty, welfare use, and teen pregnancy. Asians are lowest in all these categories. Is it wise for our immigration policies to ignore these differences?

Race is, of course, still a taboo. This is what prevents public discussion of sharp differences that would be considered grounds for national concern and even crisis if they were in areas where thinking is not constricted. Every taboo represents a subject that is removed from discussion, and this limits our understanding of the world. It is far better for Americans to understand their world—and the people who live in it—than to persist in ignorance.

Periodical Bibliography

The following articles have been selected to supplement the diverse views presented in this chapter.

Marquez Claxton	"White Justice Strikes Again," *New York Amsterdam News*, January 10, 2008.
Ifa Kamau Cush	"The Injustice of Justice," *New African*, April 2009.
Sarah B. From	"Opening the Doors of Opportunity for Women in Jail," *American Jails*, March/April 2008.
David Glenn	"Our Hidden Prejudices, on Trial," *Chronicle of Higher Education*, April 25, 2008.
Glenna Gordon	"Doing Hard Time Together," *Ms.*, Winter 2009.
Cynthia Gordy	"Extreme Lockup," *Essence*, December 2007.
Darcus Howe	"Stop-and-Search Was Never the Answer," *New Statesman*, February 11, 2008.
Dana J. Hubbard	"Getting the Most Out of Correctional Treatment: Testing the Responsivity Principle on Male and Female Offenders," *Federal Probation*, June 2007.
Dale S. Recinella	"Ending the Death Penalty," *America*, April 28, 2008.
Damon W. Root	"Sterilized by the State," *Reason*, December 2008.
Gillian Slovo	"Innocent Prisoners," *New Statesman*, September 15, 2008.
Stuart Taylor Jr.	"Criminal Injustice and Race," *National Journal*, October 6, 2007.

OPPOSING
VIEWPOINTS®
SERIES

CHAPTER 2

Should Some Criminals Be Treated Differently?

Chapter Preface

In a 2005 landmark decision, the U.S. Supreme Court ruled that "when a juvenile offender commits a heinous crime, the State can exact forfeiture of some of the most basic liberties, but the State cannot extinguish his life and his potential to attain a mature understanding of his own humanity." Up to that point, at least nineteen states made execution a possibility for minors convicted of committing serious crimes. The *Roper v. Simmons* case further ignited a discussion about the culpability of young people, calling on science to help determine when a person is old enough to understand the difference between right and wrong.

Recent research in neurobiology has led to a deeper understanding of the human brain. Sophisticated imaging equipment now reveals more about how the brain develops. Scientists at Harvard Medical School and other researchers have found that the pre-frontal cortex, the part of the brain that is responsible for decision, is the last part of the brain to develop. According to Ruben Gur, a neuroscientist at the University of Pennsylvania in Philadelphia, in a July 2004 *Science* article, the pre-frontal cortex "doesn't begin to mature until seventeen years of age. The very part of the brain that is judged by the legal system process comes on board late." Gur and other members of the medical community argue that offenders under the age of eighteen should not be put to death. Instead, they should be punished for their crime and be given the tools to be rehabilitated.

Not everyone is convinced. Skeptics argue that little evidence exists to link brain structure to human behavior. For example, in the same *Science* article, neuroscientist Elizabeth Sowell of University of California, Los Angeles (UCLA), says "we couldn't do a scan on a kid and decide if they should be tried as an adult." Still others argue that these recent conclusions only demonstrate how people use science to defend their own best interests. Dianne Clements, president of Justice for All, a victim-advocacy group, argues in a May 2004 the *Wall Street Journal* article that "there is science, and then there is junk science. This is an effort by those in the scientific community who oppose the death penalty to use science to argue their position." Opponents insist that young children know the difference from right and wrong and they should be held responsible for their actions.

Scientists will continue mapping the human brain in an attempt to link behavior to structures in the brain. For many people, this science is too new to rely on for policy making. Yet others argue it is better that the execution of juveniles has been stopped because it prevents the needless killing of young people who have a chance at becoming productive members of society. The authors in the following chapter want to ensure victims are restored to justice and criminals are punished accordingly. Determining how to treat special populations of offenders, such as the mentally ill, the elderly, and white-collar workers, however, might take extra care.

> "*Essentially these special units we're talking about are nursing homes surrounded by razor wire.*"

Older Prisoners Should Be Released Early

Barry Holman, as told to Justice Matters

Justice Matters *is published by the Partnership for Safety and Justice, an organization based in the Western United States, which seeks justice system reform. In the following viewpoint,* Justice Matters *interviews Barry Holman, senior associate of research and quality assurance of the Department of Youth Rehabilitation Services for Washington, D.C. Holman argues that the ever-growing population of older Americans in prison has created a dire human rights and economic situation. Age-related illnesses cost taxpayers money, which could be reduced if well-behaved elderly prisoners were released early.*

As you read, consider the following questions:

1. What is determinant sentencing?

2. How much more does it cost to incarcerate elderly prisoners?

"'Nursing Homes Surrounded by Razor Wire': Geriatric Prisons, an Interview with Barry Holman," *Justice Matters*, September 15, 2005. Reproduced by permission of Partnership for Safety and Justice. http://safetyandjustice.org.

3. According to the Bureau of Justice Statistics, what percentage of the U.S. prison population is over age forty-five?

From 1997–2002 Barry Holman was Research and Public Policy Director at the National Center on Institutions and Alternatives, NCIA, where he conducted research on the rising number of elderly prisoners, organized two conferences on elderly prisoners and worked with other nonprofit groups to encourage the possibility of community supervision of elderly prisoners. We interviewed Barry by phone about a new type of prison: geriatric prisons for older prisoners.

Justice Matters: We're hearing more about older prisoners these days. . . . and "geriatric prisons." When corrections officials say "geriatric prison," what age range are we talking about? Besides being older, what characteristics will the prisoners in this type of prison have?

Barry Holman: What's considered an "older" prisoner varies. Different prisons and states have different ranges varying from 50 and over to 65 and over. In some circumstances for these special units, states combine very old prisoners with the terminally ill. . . really, what we're talking about is prisoners who can't be housed in the general population, some because of age and some because they have a medical condition. There are some people in prison who are functional at age 70 or 75: they're able to get to and from the commissary. . . they can get around. They stay in general population. But there's also the very old, the frail and the very sick. Essentially these special units we're talking about are nursing homes surrounded by razor wire. . . people who need intensive nursing and assistance with daily living.

Keeping Elderly Prisoners in Jail

Wow, when you put it like that. . . help me understand. . . what's the rationale behind keeping "the very old and the frail" behind razor wire?

What I've heard from some correctional professionals is, "People have a sentence to serve, and they have to serve it in a correctional facility. Our job is to provide that facility and provide them the care they need." This sounds well-meaning, but there is a false sense that correctional staff shouldn't be involved in policy decisions. I found this quite disheartening, that—for instance—the head of a state's prison medical service felt as though they should just keep quiet and leave the decision making to others. Of course, there are some in the system who disagree. One warden from South Carolina I worked with, who had risen up the ranks from a correctional officer, he was vocally opposed to the idea of having seriously ill and elderly people in prison.

Really, this is just a function of determinant sentencing. It's about making people serve the whole sentence regardless of the circumstances. Thanks to determinant sentencing, the number of elderly prisoners is growing. Surveys of state DOCs (Departments of Corrections) show that

- In 1979 there were about 6,500 prisoners over the age of 55 (Survey of state DOCs by Bureau of Justice Statistics).

- In 1990 there were more than 19,000 prisoners over the age of 55 (Sourcebook of Corrections Stats by BJS, 1995 version).

- In 1997 there were roughly 50,000 prisoners over the age of 55 (Survey done by NCIA). The survey that we did at NCIA (National Center on Institutions and Alternatives) in 1997 showed that there had been a tremendous increase in the number of older prisoners—a seven-fold increase over the course of a generation. And a majority of all these prisoners over 55—just over half—were in for non-violent convictions. In the federal system, though, 97% of prisoners over 55 were serving time for non-violent convictions.

After the study I was involved with an effort to pull together a pilot project. We would've moved some elderly prisoners out of correctional settings into community-based supervision and care. Some of them might have wound up in a nursing home with security, or some in intensive supervision while they resided with family or other community members. The idea was to do individualized planning based on their specific security and care needs.

Sounds interesting. . . but it doesn't sound like it happened.

No, it didn't. This was a pilot project for the federal system, and we heard from Senators who wanted to know which prisoners from their state might wind up in the demonstration project. The concern was that it might look bad for them later if they approved it.

The perception is that "There's a sentence and we have to stick with it no matter what." There are public relations concerns about releasing any prisoner, no matter how minor the crime. There's also a fear that we would be facing a situation similar to what happened in the 1980s, when people were dumped out of mental health institutions and out onto the street. The argument is that at least in prison they're getting care, maybe even better care than they would be getting in the community. But the idea that we're doing them a favor by keeping them inside is perverse.

Caring for Elderly Prisoners

But we are concerned that people who need medical care should get it. How does care for the sick or the frail in prison compare to what they could get on the outside?

If you put sick people on a bus and dump them homeless on the street . . . well, yes, they would be in trouble. But if you do case planning to deal with security and medical needs, organize an appropriate place to stay and connect them with other supports, that's different. The pilot project was going to be with low-level offenders and we wanted to incorporate better supervision. You can save a lot of money by keeping people

State and Federal Inmates Age 50+ (1992–2001)

Year	Inmates
1992	41,586
1993	44,302
1994	50,478
1995	55,281
1996	63,004
1997	73,543
1998	83,667
1999	92,362
2000	103,132
2001	113,358

Source of Statistics: Anno, B. Jaye, Camilia Graham, James E. Lawrence, and Ronald Shansky. *Correctional Health Care: Addressing the Needs of Elderly, Chronically Ill and Terminally Ill Inmates.* U.S. Department of Justice/National Institute of Justice, 2004.

TAKEN FROM: Carrie Abner, "Graying Prisons: States Face Challenges of an Aging Inmate Population," *State News*, Council of State Governments, November/December 2006, www.csg.org.

in the least restrictive place possible. Plus there's just the human side of it. Talk to any older prisoner and their biggest fear is that they're going to die behind bars.

It doesn't have to be prison every time for everyone. We're better served on a number of fronts if we were smarter with these dollars. The cost of incarcerating elderly prisoners is triple the cost of the average prisoner. It's very inefficient to house the very sick and very old in prison. . . take for example, a rural facility that has someone who needs dialysis. The transportation costs for that are high. Now for some, that becomes an argument for a central prison with all the most ill prisoners. . . so it can be done cheaper. . . but beyond the cost there's just the inhumanity of it. This type of thinking has nothing to do with public safety or what's really the appropriate way to treat people, it makes them a commodity and dehumanizes them.

To take that example you just used, some people are very functional on dialysis. Certainly just because someone is old doesn't mean they can't be very active. We can't explain this as just "these folks are helpless because they have a medical condition or because they're old."

Yes, which comes back to the need for individualized planning. Does it make sense to have this person here? Does it further public safety? Is it a good use of public funds?

Making Individual Assessments

Let's say, though, we're not talking about people with drug or theft convictions, but maybe a prisoner who's serving a life sentence for murder or another serious crime. I'm one of these people in a situation where someone is serving a life sentence for murdering a member of my family. I can totally understand how it could be hard for a surviving family member of a murder victim to hear about a person convicted for that murder getting "out early" to be moved to a nursing home. What would you say about those situations?

First, it's important to note what I'm talking about doesn't automatically mean releasing people early. We're talking about individual assessments based on a number of factors, including the nature of the situation, the opinion of mental health experts. . . people looking closely at how well this person could function safely in the community and whether or not they pose a threat.

And we also know that causing someone else to suffer doesn't make up for suffering that was caused to someone in the past. It just can't. There aren't simple ways to just end people's pain. Healing doesn't come from the suffering of another person. There might be a role for victims' family members or survivors in that process, and the prisoner themselves, to assess the risk and determine which way to go. We need to get beyond formulaic justice that doesn't help anyone and needlessly hurts many.

Recently the Bureau of Justice Statistics released statistics on reported deaths in state prisons and jails. They said prisoners over the age of 45 make up less than 20% of the prison population (17%, actually), but are two-thirds of people dying in prison. And it's possible that this report has substantially under-counted deaths inside, so the problem might be even greater than that. What does that statistic tell us?

Well, first that report tells us there are too many people dying in prison. If someone's been sentenced to a life sentence without possible parole, then we can expect that person will eventually die in prison. There will be accidents and unexpected deaths. We expect a small number of those. But we should expect people with non-violent convictions, who don't pose a public safety risk and can be supervised and served in the community, they should not be dying in prison from disease or illness. That's just a travesty. It's a question for our conscience.

Like the US population as a whole, the prison population is aging quickly. Unless we change our policies, our laws and our attitudes toward them, many will needlessly languish and die in prison for decades to come.

"*Releasing a once violent criminal gives others incentive to evade the law the best they can.*"

Older Prisoners Should Not Receive Lenient Sentences

Kelly Porcella

Kelly Porcella is an associate managing editor of the St. John's Law Review *and a graduate student at St. John's University School of Law. In the following viewpoint, she argues that elderly criminals should not receive lenient sentences based solely on their age. Although housing older inmates can be costly, Porcella asserts that it is a miscarriage of justice to give them shorter sentences than their younger counterparts. She also notes that releasing older prisoners early sends the wrong message to victims, their families, and potential criminals.*

As you read, consider the following questions:

1. What is the average annual cost of housing an elderly prisoner?

2. What is the basic message stated by the Eighth Amendment?

Kelly Porcella, "The Past Coming Back to Haunt Them: The Prosecution and Sentencing of Once Deadly but Now Elderly Criminals," *St. John's Law Review*, vol. 81, Winter 2007, pp. 369–97. Copyright © 2007 St. John's Law Review. Reproduced by permission.

3. What three reasons are given by the court in *United States v. Angiulo* for why long prison sentences might be more difficult for younger offenders?

When an eighty-year-old man in a wheelchair and on oxygen is wheeled past any citizen on a sidewalk, sympathy for his plight is surely felt. When the same man is wheeled into a courtroom to stand trial for the murder of three young men forty years ago, a difference of opinion emerges. The debate is between those who see the aging defendant as he is today and argue to let the past remain the past, and those who see the defendant as he was in the past and urge that justice must be done today. Does an elderly person who took a life so much earlier in his or her own life deserve our sympathy, and as a result, leniency? This Note argues no. . . .

Low Risk to the Public

A key argument for the lenient sentencing of elderly convicts is that they pose only a nominal threat to society—both presently and in the future. Illustrative of this point is that elderly prisoners in general have a very low risk of escape. [According to Donald Newman, sociologist at the State University of New York at Albany] "[N]o matter what the elderly criminals did, they don't need handcuffs, leg irons and a 30-foot wall. . . ." Similarly, older offenders have the lowest risk of recidivism. Only about one percent of released elderly inmates are ever convicted of another crime, and the sickly elderly person is the least likely to ever commit another crime.

This public safety argument is not persuasive when posed toward elderly evaders because of the severity of their crimes. Even if an elderly evader would not commit another crime as drastic as murder, if that person is not sufficiently punished for the first one, he or she is actually given "one free kill." Additionally, another important goal of sentencing is to send a message to others considering committing similar crimes that there will be consequences for their actions. For example, in *State v. Baker*, the defendant was convicted of voluntary manslaughter. Due to his advanced age and declining physical condition, he argued that he was not a risk to society and would therefore be appropriately punished through probation. The court disagreed, stating that such a lesser punishment "would be saying to the community that it is okay to take another's life."

Elderly Inmates Are Costly

Related to their low risk to the public, the cost of incarcerating older criminals is a widely-cited argument for more lenient sentences or alternate punishment methods. Elderly inmates do not require the same safety measures that prisons use when dealing with younger inmates; therefore, society should not have to pay for these measures to be applied to them. As former Attorney General Janet Reno contended, "you don't want to be running a geriatric ward at age 75 or 80 for people who are no longer dangerous." In effect, housing elderly inmates only serves to contribute to the already overcrowded prison system.

The average annual cost of confining an elderly prisoner is estimated to be between sixty and seventy thousand dollars. Driven by the special medical needs of older inmates, this figure is at least three times the cost spent to incarcerate younger inmates and more than double that of running a nursing home. In Oklahoma, inmate medical care costs are double the cost of food and five times the cost of utilities. It is no wonder that it has been said [by Richard Gray, a district attorney in Oklahoma] that "[t]he last years of life are the most expensive."

Some claim that the elderly have access to services outside prison, such as specialized transportation, which improve their quality of life and do not cost the taxpayer. Reduced sentences and alternative forms of punishment for elderly and infirm prisoners, then, might be as efficient and less costly. Such alternatives include pardons, medical releases, electronic home detention, probation, parole, and specialized housing.

The first rebuttal to this cost argument lies in the reality of government taxing and spending: Whether an elderly person is in prison or outside paying for services such as special transportation through Medicare, Medicaid, or Social Security, the public is still paying for their care through taxes. A second, retributivist counterpoint dealing specifically with elderly evaders is that alternative sentences to imprisonment might not be punishment enough; in other words, they would not be proportionate to the crime. Sentencers determine who will be given an alternative form of punishment based on the risk that they pose to society. As elderly offenders are usually determined to be a small risk to the community, they are given lower risk ratings *regardless of the offense committed,* and are consequently more lightly supervised. Under these circumstances, even a person who killed someone and then evaded the law for decades could get no more than light supervision as punishment. In addition, family-based supervision, another form of punishment, may be in effect "no supervision," when the elderly evaders' families shield them from the consequences of their criminal conduct. Quite the opposite, younger criminals are being sentenced to long prison terms for crimes less serious than murder. If they learn that older evaders receive lesser sentences even for harsher crimes, these young criminals will just do their best to avoid being prosecuted.

Short Life Expectancy

"So the defendant said to the judge [upon sentencing], 'I'm 65 years old. I don't think I can do that much time.' So the judge said, 'Do the best you can.'" This anecdote, though amusing, demonstrates an important point: The life expectancy of a de-

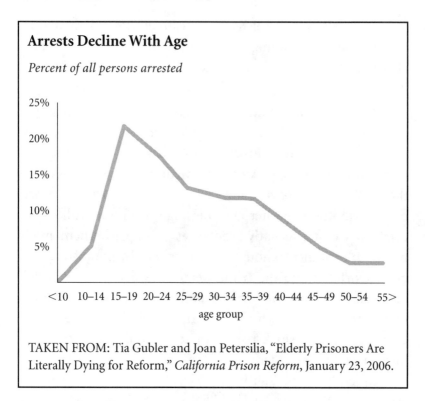

Arrests Decline With Age

Percent of all persons arrested

TAKEN FROM: Tia Gubler and Joan Petersilia, "Elderly Prisoners Are Literally Dying for Reform," *California Prison Reform*, January 23, 2006.

fendant is immaterial to sentencing. As put another way, "'senior citizens are entitled to discounts to movies' not in [sentencing]."

Proponents of proportionality in sentencing argue that the same sentence is more severe for an older person than a younger person since the older person would be forced to spend a greater percentage of his or her remaining life behind bars. In fact, any sentence might constitute life imprisonment for the elderly prisoner. To preserve proportionality, the elderly should instead be sentenced to periods that represent the same percentages of their remaining lives as do the sentences imposed on younger offenders.

This proportionality argument is unpersuasive for several reasons. First, if it were persuasive, terminally ill patients would have "a license to kill," a license to hurt someone without being punished for very long, if at all. [According to the

United States v. Willis,] "[Proportionality] should not amount to a 'get out of jail free' card for defendants of a certain age or with certain conditions." In the case of elderly evaders, it would appear that a more logical proportionality scheme would calculate the criminal's remaining life from the date of the crime, not the date of sentencing. Otherwise, criminals are encouraged to evade the law.

Second, although a defendant may argue that a sentence amounting to life in prison is disproportionate to his or her crime, cases in which defendants challenged sentences on Eighth Amendment "Cruel and Unusual Punishment" grounds have been unsuccessful. In *Harmelin v. Michigan*, the Supreme Court held that the Eighth Amendment only prohibits "grossly disproportionate" sentences, of which life in prison is not one.

Third, the process that courts would use to predict life expectancy if they had to take into account an evader's remaining life would be problematic and impractical. For example, in *People v. Moore*, the court stated that trial courts would be "reviewing the life expectancies of demographic subgroups, family health histories, and behavioral risks of acquiring certain illnesses, such as cancer and heart disease." Such analysis might be futile anyway because anyone could die at any time—even shorter sentences could amount to longer than an offender's actual life. Similarly, when Edgar Ray Killen was freed pending appeal after being sentenced for three counts of manslaughter, victims' friends and families worried that he might die before ever going to prison; justice would never had been done had he died a free man.

Finally, making individualized life expectancy a factor would raise possible Equal Protection problems. Although a court may be sympathetic toward aging defendants who will or may spend the rest of their lives in prison, [according to *State v. Belanger,*] "sympathy cannot properly serve as a basis for a modification of a sentence," because, if it did, punishments would be applied inequitably at the discretion of the court.

Inability to Adapt to Prison Life

Retributivist proponents of lenient sentencing argue that if a younger prisoner and an older prisoner are each given the same sentence, the older prisoner will suffer more for each year in prison because the prison environment is harsher on older inmates than on younger ones. To ensure proportionality and account for that difference, proponents argue the elderly should receive lesser or alternative sentences or special treatment in prison.

The prison environment can be unkind for an elderly prisoner. Elderly prisoners are less able than younger prisoners to cope with problems caused by prison design; they have trouble with the noise and fast pace of prison and may have difficulty walking up and down stairs and walking distances within the prison building itself. They are also susceptible to the aggressive acts of younger prisoners, including threats and attacks. Still, elderly prisoners are not usually given special treatment in prison. Most elderly inmates spend their time in the mainstream prison system; they are not separated or given lighter work assignments unless they are also sick.

In addition to physical health, mental health is also an issue for elderly inmates. Older prisoners generally demonstrate very high stress levels. Some proponents of reduced sentences argue that individuals near the end of their lives feel compelled to get their affairs in order before they die, that a prison sentence prevents them from doing so, and thus causes mental suffering.

Alternatively, an elderly person's life outside prison may be unfulfilling or so similar to prison life that he or she may suffer less than a younger inmate. The court in *United States v. Angiulo* stated that the argument that a sentence falls more harshly upon an elderly offender is "an untested conclusion, unsupported by any psychological or sociological analysis." In fact, the court suggested that the opposite might be true— long prison sentences are more adverse for young offenders who will probably be unable to marry, be a parent, or have a career.

Ultimately, each offender, young or old, has an individualized prison experience based on their different emotional and physical characteristics and their former social role. Moreover, each prison provides its own unique environment that shapes an inmate's daily living. Any argument that concludes that prison life is necessarily harsher for older inmates because of their age fails to take these factors into account and perpetuates the stereotype of the weak older person. The impossibility of predicting what prison life will be like for each and every criminal makes the best sentencing system one of clarity, a system where sentencing remains constant across a population of similar criminals, regardless of their age. . . .

Arguments Remain Unconvincing

The essential question is whether elderly evaders' low risk to the public, high cost of incarceration, short life expectancy, inability to adapt to prison life, and contributions to society outweigh the need for general deterrence, proportionality between the crime and the punishment, uniformity in sentencing, and vindication of victims' rights. The answer is no.

The arguments for lenient sentencing are just not strong enough. Releasing a once violent criminal who successfully evaded the law for decades based on the fact he or she can no longer hurt anyone gives others incentive to evade the law the best they can. In the case of a murderer, especially, the cost of incarceration is not outweighed by the gravity of this "most heinous" offense. In addition, requiring courts to estimate an evader's life expectancy in sentencing would be impractical, inequitable, and not that useful, considering than any day could be anyone's last. Moreover, there is no proof that the prison environment is necessarily harsher on older criminals than on younger criminals; the opposite might be true. Finally, it is unjust to use the elderly evaders' contributions to society to reduce their sentences; people from their generation who were actually caught and imprisoned never had that opportunity and for that reason were shown no such leniency.

The arguments against lenient sentencing are more convincing. Incarcerating an elderly evader sends the message to others who evade the law that although it might be delayed, justice will be done. Also, time behind bars reflects the gravity of the offense. Additionally, imprisonment of the elderly evader is the least that can be done to strive toward uniformity in sentencing. Ultimately, not sufficiently punishing an elderly evader continues the injustice that the evader has done to victims and their families.

> "The mental health personage usually argues for mitigation, not elimination, of punishment."

Mentally Ill Offenders Should Be Held Responsible for Their Actions

Richard E. Vatz

Richard E. Vatz is an editor of USA Today *and* Current Psychology *and professor of rhetoric at Towson University in Maryland. In the following viewpoint, he argues that mental health experts are too quick to designate criminals as insane. He asserts that some criminals have knowingly committed crimes while in prison to prove their insanity so that they can serve time in a psychiatric hospital rather than in prison. Vatz notes by attempting to prove their clients are "not guilty by reason of insanity," psychiatrists are simply providing criminals with the means for escaping punishment.*

As you read, consider the following questions:

1. What is a PET scan?

Richard E. Vatz, "Accommodating the Killer," *USA Today Magazine*, September 2008, pp. 22–23. Copyright © 2008 Society for the Advancement of Education. Reproduced by permission.

2. What is the American Psychiatric Association's stance on mental health experts and determining criminal responsibility?

3. How often is the insanity plea successful in court?

Of all of the matters that psychiatrists, psychologists, and social workers undertake, support of accused criminals', and particularly killers', pleas of "not guilty by reason of insanity" or, in some states, "not criminally responsible," is perhaps the most outrageously invalid. Many of their clients or patients are voluntary. Whatever debates exist concerning the prescribing of psychoactive drugs, such activities usually are desired by the recipients. Whatever role mental health practitioners play in adjudicating interpersonal legal disputes, at least they theoretically can bring the concept of "the reasonable man" (now, perhaps, the reasonable person) to hear without resorting to creating exculpatory bases for others' derelictions of responsibility in decision making. Even when testifying in court regarding the penalty phase after a verdict has been rendered, the mental health personage usually argues for mitigation, not elimination, of punishment.

Getting Out of Prison Time

When defense mental health "experts" testify to a lack of a defendant's criminal intent, these "hired guns" are aiming to have the perpetrator confined to a psychiatric institution rather than a jail. In some cases, a murderer who is in prison for life without parole, as was the case early in 2008 for Maryland's Kevin Johns, can kill again with the hope of being found insane or not criminally responsible and, therefore, be taken out of horrible prison confines and placed in a different location for incarceration. Moreover, what if this prisoner is in a state (which he is in Maryland) that effectively has eliminated executions—not by law, but by practice? In short, what does a rational murderer who faces life imprisonment without the possibility of parole, but not execution (regardless of what he does), potentially do to improve his lot?

He murders again and, if he has a history of being violent in a repeated and unconventional way, he specifically may avoid going to—or escape—Supermax prison (in Baltimore, [Maryland]) and instead get sent to a relatively more pleasant psychiatric facility. This arguably was the motive in Johns' brutal killing of Philip E. Parker Jr. on a prison bus. Johns has had a long, violent history, culminating in the killing of Parker in February 2005. The judge, Emory A. Plitt Jr., originally decided in June of 2008 that Johns was "not criminally responsible." The appalled concern of many was that this decision would allow Johns to be placed in a psychiatric facility wherein no one could guarantee that his violence could be quelled. In addition, such a legal outcome would appear to be a direct reward for the murderer's killing again and perhaps precisely that for which he was aiming.

Judge Plitt may have redeemed himself slightly by subsequently deciding to let the Maryland Department of Health and Mental Hygiene determine that Johns receive psychiatric care at Supermax prison rather than at Clifton T. Perkins Hospital, the first time such a determination has been made for someone who has received such a verdict. Again, though, there is a much more important issue not answered by the bench's surprise decision that eliminated Johns' efforts to avoid Supermax: why would psychiatrists and then a judge conclude that a killer whose crime may benefit him could not appreciate the criminality of his conduct or conform that conduct to the requirements of the law—the criteria by which a perpetrator may be found "not criminally responsible" in Maryland or "not guilty by reason of insanity" in other states?

The prosecutor in the Johns case, S. Ann Brobst, put it perfectly: "He doesn't care if he gets caught. He was just sentenced to life without parole. . . . He has nothing to lose by killing someone else. He has everything to gain."

Using the Insanity Defense

- Approximately 1% of defendants who are charged with a felony plead insanity, and only 15% to 25% of those who plead insanity are actually found not guilty by reason of insanity. Juries are significantly less likely to render an insanity verdict than are judges.

- Defendants with a history of major mental illness and who had psychiatric hospitalizations had higher rates of acquittal by reason of insanity than those without such a history.

- Subjective moral wrongfulness refers to the act of a defendant who commits an offense with knowledge that the act is illegal but who believes it is personally morally justified. In contrast, objective moral wrongfulness refers to the act of a defendant who, as a result of a psychiatric disorder, lacks the capacity to know that society considers his or her act to be wrong.

James L. Knoll IV and Phillip J. Resnick,
"Insanity Defense Evaluations,"
Psychiatric Times, *vol. 25, no. 14, December 1, 2008.*

Melissa Rodriguez, the mother of Parker, who was serving a short sentence for committing a robbery with a pellet gun, was outraged, but virtually ignored, as too often is the case with deceased victims' relatives. She said tellingly in front of television cameras, "Everything's about Kevin, Kevin, Kevin. . . . I hope this judge realizes what he's done. [The victim] next time may be a guard."

David Williamson, a psychologist, testified for the defense, and—true to all insufficiently ethically concerned insanity defense lawyers—said without evidence that Johns' symptoms were difficult to fake. Then again, so were Vincent Gigante's. Gigante was the reputed leader of the nation's largest criminal organization, the Genovese family. For decades, Gigante walked around talking crazily to telephone polls. A group of very prestigious forensic psychiatrists from top American universities claimed for the defense that there was no way he could be faking mental illness. He was, one said on *60 Minutes*, "exactly the kind of patient we see in a dementia clinic." In addition, nationally-recognized neuropsychiatrist Monte Buchsbaum insisted that a Positron Emission Tomography (PET) scan proved Gigante's incompetence to stand trial. Gigante walked into a courtroom in 2003 and conceded via a plea agreement that he had been faking it all along.

The Job of Psychiatrists?

Was Johns aware of what he was doing? He openly predicted he would kill again. A long history of particularly brutal, unconventionally violent behavior should not be used as evidence that a person is not responsible for what he or she does. The American Psychiatric Association itself a few years ago had on its Web site the statement that it "is the job of the judge or jury [not psychiatrists] to determine criminal responsibility." To the knowledge of this writer, no mental health expert ever has been asked publicly to reconcile this statement with the practice of testifying for those who plead insanity. Besides, "insanity" is not an accepted psychiatric concept. In the Johns case, the judge fumbled and gave additional hope to killers trying to avoid prison, notwithstanding his refusal to send Johns to a psychiatric facility.

Simultaneous with this case, talk radio in Maryland, along with other media outlets, sporadically were discussing the possible ramifications of Johns' succeeding in his possible goal of relocating his incarceration venue at no cost to him. If Peter Finley Dunne's Mr. Dooley's dictum that "the Supreme Court follows the election returns" is true, one only can hope that public outrage at the undermining of the criminal justice system with strategic uses of the insanity plea will serve to lessen such attempts. The outrage over the successful plea of not guilty by reason of insanity by John Hinckley—[President] Ronald Reagan's would-be assassin—led to tighter control over such pleas and specifically the change in Federal courts to the presumption being that the accused is not legally insane. It was the opposite for Hinckley in the early 1980s when his plea, once accepted by the judge, acquired a presumption of truth that may have led to its success.

Forensic psychiatrists are prone to point out that the insanity plea is successful in only one out of every 400 attempts. Such statistics, while literally true, ignore the excusing effect of psychiatry in the courtroom and hide the fact that, while relatively small, that success rate translates into thousands of cases over the years.

The outcome of perhaps an even more upsetting case is pending in Maryland. Mark Castillo, age 41, was engaged in a long-term custody battle with his wife. She had filed court motions for months pleading that he not be allowed access to their children. He taunted and threatened his wife (in later publicly publicized recordings), telling her that one way he really could get to her would be to kill her offspring. On March 30, 2008, he did just that, ending the lives of their children Anthony, Austin, and Athena—ages six, four, and two, respectively. In the early afternoon at a downtown hotel, the site of the killings, he contacted hotel security saying what he had done and threatening to commit suicide. His efforts regarding ending his own life were less successful and perhaps less eager.

Neighbors, not particularly surprisingly, described Castillo as a friendly guy—one even calling him "an excellent father"—as is not infrequently the case with violent family perpetrators. Despite the clarity of the expressed motive by the killer to make the mother, pediatrician Amy Castillo, "live without them," Castillo pleaded "not criminally responsible."

He likely will not find it difficult to engage psychiatric forensic "experts" to help him make his case. As for his prosecution, psychiatrists in the Circuit Court Medical Services Division of Baltimore will be making a recommendation to the court as to the criminal responsibility of Castillo. Prosecutors have given mixed signals as to whether they will accept that recommendation or contest the plea, if necessary, but their most recent statements (as of this writing [September 2008]) imply they will seek criminal punishment regardless of what the psychiatrists recommend. [In January 2009, a judge agreed to delay Castillo's trial until April 2009 after the defense asked to argue he was not criminally responsible for the killings.]

When psychiatrically suspect findings are nationally publicized, such as in the Hinckley case, the public often puts pressure on the criminal justice system to toughen up. However, the more local the case, no matter how transparent the motive, the less likely the public will demand condign punishment, even if we end up giving license to the murder of defenseless children. Public pressure, on the other hand, may have affected the Johns outcome positively, and perhaps there even might be a small—albeit very small—trend in this regard.

| *"There is an increasing recognition that severe mental illness is a reason to spare people not from responsibility for their crimes, but from the ultimate sanction of death."*

Mentally Ill Offenders Should Not Be Executed

American Civil Liberties Union

The American Civil Liberties Union (ACLU) is a national organization that works to protect human rights. In the following viewpoint, the ACLU argues that mentally ill criminals should not be executed. Evidence supports that many people, including judges and jurors, misunderstand mental illness, which can lead to a person without a clear understanding of right and wrong being put to death. Given that mental illness is caused by disorders of the brain, the ACLU implores that the United States stop executing mentally ill offenders, which is in keeping with most nations' and international laws.

American Civil Liberties Union, "Mental Illness and the Death Penalty in the United States," January 31, 2005. Reproduced by permission. www.aclu.org.

As you read, consider the following questions:

1. According to the Bureau of Justice Statistics, in 1998 how many mentally ill offenders were incarcerated in prison or jail?

2. What was the ruling of the 1986 Supreme Court case *Ford v. Wainwright*?

3. Which three major international policies respond to the rights of the mentally ill on death row?

There are significant gaps in the legal protection accorded severely mentally ill defendants charged with or convicted of a capital crime. Most notably, this country still permits the execution of the severely mentally ill. The problem is not a small one. A leading mental health group, Mental Health America, estimates that five to ten percent of all death row inmates suffer from a severe mental illness.

This overview discusses the intersection of the law and the challenges faced by mentally ill capital defendants at every stage from trial through appeals and execution. It provides examples of some of the more famous cases of the execution of the mentally ill. Lastly, it describes current legislative efforts to exempt those who suffer from a serious mental illness from execution and the importance of such efforts.

I. Mental Illness and Capital Trials

Since 1976, all capital trials in the United States are divided into two phases. At the first phase, the question is whether the defendant is guilty or innocent of the charged offense. If the defendant is found guilty at the first phase of a murder that is eligible for the death penalty in that jurisdiction, the defendant will then face the second phase. In the penalty phase of the trial, the jury will decide whether to recommend a life sentence or a death sentence for the defendant.

Mental illness is relevant to numerous important legal questions at capital trials, including:

(1) POLICE INTERROGATION. Those suffering from a mental illness can be more vulnerable to police pressure and more likely to give false confessions. Empirical studies demonstrate that the following characteristics associated with mental illness can lead to false confessions: impulsivity, deficits in cognitive processing, suggestibility, delusions and extreme compliance. Other studies demonstrate that mentally ill defendants (who are not mentally retarded) have significant difficulties understanding the Miranda rights against self-incrimination and access to an attorney that they are asked to waive during police interrogation. Thus, people with mental illness facing police interrogation are more likely to waive rights they do not understand and more likely to falsely confess.

(2) COMPETENCY TO STAND TRIAL. A defendant must be "competent" to stand trial under the United States Constitution. A competency hearing determines whether a defendant has "a rational as well as factual understanding of the proceedings" and whether the defendant has "ability to consult with his lawyer with a reasonable degree of rational understanding." For example, a defendant with schizophrenia who has such severe delusions that he or she has lost contact with reality and cannot meaningfully consult with his or her lawyer should be declared incompetent to stand trial.

In reality, the competency test as applied by courts is a low bar and courts or juries routinely find that severely mentally ill defendants, including capital defendants, meet the basic test of competency. In other words, just because a defendant is schizophrenic, or delusional, does not mean that he or she will be found incompetent to stand trial.

If a trial judge concludes that a capital defendant is incompetent to stand trial, the defendant will typically be transferred to a state mental hospital where the state doctors will try to improve the defendant's mental state so that he or she can meet the competency standard. In *Sell v. United States*,

539 U.S. 166 (2003), the Supreme Court set clear rules about when a defendant who is not dangerous to himself or to others may be forcibly medicated against his or her will for the purpose of rendering the defendant competent to stand trial. Under *Sell*, forcible medication must be limited to those "rare" circumstances where the medication is: (1) medically appropriate; (2) unlikely to have side effects that undermine the fairness of the trial; and (3) necessary to significantly further important government trial-related interests, after taking into account other available alternatives. Under these rules, for example, the government should not be able to force a defendant to receive medication if counseling might be a possible alternative or if side effects from the medication would render the defendant unable to participate meaningfully in his or her defense at trial.

(3) INSANITY. Although there are important differences among the states, insanity is usually a defense to the crime that must be raised and proved by the defense. The most common insanity test, the "M'Naghten test," asks whether the defendant was unable to understand what he or she was doing at the time of the crime due to some "defect of reason or disease of the mind" or, if he or she was aware of what she was doing, that he or she failed to understand that what he or she was doing was wrong. The American Law Institute test is the second most commonly used test for insanity. The ALI test asks whether the defendant lacks substantial capacity either to appreciate the criminality of his conduct or to conform his conduct to the requirements of law as a result of a mental disease or defect.

Under either test, juries frequently reject insanity defenses in capital cases despite strong evidence that the defendants were suffering from serious mental illnesses at the time of the crime. Part of the explanation is the fear created in the public was from the high profile acquittal of John Hinckley, Jr. on insanity grounds after he attempted to assassinate President

Ronald Reagan. In some states, the legislatures responded to the backlash against insanity defenses by creating a new verdict, "guilty but mentally ill." Unfortunately, many jurors are unaware that a "guilty but mentally ill" verdict is virtually identical to a "guilty" verdict for defendants, and a capital defendant who is found "guilty but mentally ill" can still face the death penalty and execution.

(4) ABILITY TO FORM CRIMINAL INTENT. Most capital murder statutes require that the State prove beyond a reasonable doubt that the defendant specifically intended to kill the victim. However, many capital defendants who suffer from serious mental illness lacked the capacity to form a specific intent to kill at the time of their offense. In a troubling decision, *Clark v. Arizona,* 548 U.S. 735 (2006), the United States Supreme Court held that such defendants do not have a constitutional right to present evidence that they suffered from a serious mental illness to show that they did not have specific intent to kill. In dissent, Justice Kennedy declared: "In my submission the Court is incorrect in holding that Arizona may convict petitioner Eric Clark of first-degree murder for the intentional or knowing killing of a police officer when Clark was not permitted to introduce critical and reliable evidence showing he did not have that intent or knowledge."

(5) MITIGATION. Evidence of mental illness may be critically important for capital defendants at the penalty phase of their trials. At the penalty phase, the defendant is constitutionally entitled to present "mitigating evidence," or any evidence that would serve as a basis for a life verdict. For example, the defendant can introduce evidence that he or she was severely abused as a child as mitigating evidence.

Although mental health evidence can be powerful mitigation, research has shown that jurors often misunderstand the relationship between mental illness and mitigating factors. All too often, jurors treat mental illness as a reason to vote for death, rather than a reason to vote for life.

(6) ADDITIONAL ISSUES AT CAPITAL TRIALS. Mentally ill defendants face other unique challenges throughout the trial process. Because of their mental illnesses, they may distrust their lawyers and have difficulty participating in their defenses. Often, mentally ill capital defendants fire their lawyers and represent themselves or waive their appeals. The same system of delusional beliefs that fundamentally prevents some severely mentally ill defendants from being able to present a rational defense may lead those defendants to fervently believe that they, and they alone, are capable of defending themselves at trial.

In addition, if they are not medicated, their demeanor and behavior at trial may frighten jurors and serve as another basis for death. On the other hand, strong doses of anti-psychotic drugs have known sedating properties and may causes defendants to appear at trial as if they don't care about the case or as zombies. The law provides little to no protection for these problems faced by the mentally ill.

II. Mental Illness and Executions

While the Supreme Court of the United States prohibited the execution of people with mental retardation in the case of *Atkins v. Virginia*, 536 U.S. 304 (2002), it has not yet ruled that it is unconstitutional to execute someone who suffered from a serious mental illness at the time of the crime. The Court has, however, stated that it is unconstitutional to execute someone who is incompetent at the time of his or her execution. The Supreme Court has visited the issue of mental incompetence in two important cases.

In *Ford v. Wainwright*, 477 U.S. 399 (1986), the Court held that it was unconstitutional to execute someone who was incompetent at the time of his execution. In a famous concurring opinion, Justice Lewis Powell laid out the test for prohibiting the execution of a person who has been incompetent. Justice Powell stated the "Eighth Amendment forbids the ex-

The Death Penalty Disregards Mental Illness

The execution of those with mental illness or "the insane" is clearly prohibited by international law. Virtually every country in the world prohibits the execution of people with mental illness.

International Resolution	Year	Excerpt
UN Safeguards Guaranteeing Protection of the Rights of Those Facing the Death Penalty	1984	" . . . nor shall the death sentence be carried out . . . on persons who have become insane."

Amnesty International USA,
"Abolish the Death Penalty:
The Death Penalty Disregards Mental Illness," 2007.
www.amnestyusa.org.

ecution only of those who are unaware of the punishment they are about to suffer and why they are to suffer it."

In *Panetti v. Quarterman*, 127 S. Ct. 2842 (2007), the Supreme Court reaffirmed that a defendant can not be executed if he is incompetent at the time of his execution and clarified the *Ford* standard. Panetti's lawyers argued that Panetti was not given an opportunity to show that he was not competent to be executed. The Texas judge presiding over the case had appointed experts to determine Panetti's competence but did not give Panetti's attorneys the opportunity to present defense experts. The Supreme Court agreed with Panetti and held that he did not receive his due process rights to a fair competency hearing. The Supreme Court also clarified what it means to be competent to be executed and held that a defendant must have a "rational understanding of the reason for the execution." This was important in Panetti's case because the lower court had concluded that Panetti needed only to know the "the fact of his impending execution and factual predicate for the execution." The parties agreed that Panetti knew that he committed two murders and knew that Texas wanted to execute him. Panetti also believed, however, that the true reason why Texas was seeking his execution was because he was preaching the Gospel. The Supreme Court explained that if a defendant is suffering from such a serious delusion that he does not understand the link between his crime and the execution, "the punishment can serve no proper purpose."

The United States Supreme Court has not yet addressed whether a state may forcibly medicate a mentally-ill defendant in order to make them competent to be executed. There is no consensus on the issue in the lower courts. One federal court of appeals decision, *Singleton v. Norris*, 319 F.3d 1018 (8th Cir. 2003) (en banc), permitted the State of Arkansas to continue to forcibly medicate a death row inmate with an impending execution date on the ground that the medication was necessary to the safety of the defendant and other inmates. The inmate, Charles Singleton, suffered from paranoid schizophrenia and without the medication would not have been competent and could not have been executed. After the United States Supreme Court refused to hear the appeal, Mr. Singleton was forcibly medicated and executed in 2004. The *Singleton* decision was heavily criticized because the court of appeals refused to consider the fact that the medication would permit his execution in the calculation when deciding whether the medication was "appropriate medical care."

State supreme court decisions in South Carolina and Louisiana, however, have recognized that the forcible medication of a mentally-ill defendant is unconstitutional. The Louisiana Supreme Court eloquently explained this conclusion:

The punishment intended for Perry [the defendant] is severely degrading to human dignity. It will involve far more than the mere extinguishment of human life. Unlike other death row prisoners, Perry will be forced to yield to the state the control of his mind, thoughts and bodily functions, ingest or absorb powerful toxic chemicals, and risk or suffer harmful, possibly fatal, drug side effects. He will not be afforded a humane exit but will suffer unique indignities and degradation. In fact, he will be forced to linger for a protracted period, stripped of the vestiges of humanity and dignity usually reserved to death row inmates, with the growing awareness that the state is converting his own mind and body into a vehicle for his execution. In short, Perry will be treated as a thing, rather than a human being, and deliberately subjected to "something inhuman, barbarous" and analogous to torture.

Maryland has solved the problem of forcibly medicating the condemned by statute. Under Maryland law, if a defendant is found to be incompetent to be executed, the trial court must commute the death sentence to a life without parole sentence. This law eliminates the possibility of forcibly medicating for any purpose other than what is truly "appropriate medical care" for the inmate.

III. Executions of People with Mental Disorders

Numerous capital inmates suffering from serious mental illnesses have been executed. Kelsey Patterson was executed by Texas in 2004. Patterson had a history of committing violent crimes but being found incompetent because he was diagnosed with paranoid schizophrenia. He voluntarily committed himself to a hospital after one crime. Despite his history and diagnosis, Patterson was found competent to stand trial by a jury after two murders in 1992. Patterson talked about conspiracies against him during his capital trial. Even though the Texas Board of Pardons and Paroles recommended that

Patterson's death sentence be commuted to life, the governor did not follow the recommendation.

Pernell Ford was executed in Alabama in 2000. During the capital trial, Ford acted as his own counsel. While presenting his "defense", Ford wanted the victims of the crime to be brought into the courtroom so that God could resurrect them.

Viet Nam veteran Manny Babbitt was executed by California in 1999. Babbitt suffered from Post-Traumatic Stress Disorder as a result of his military service. The details of his crime indicate he had a flashback to war. He wrapped his victim in a blanket and tagged her as he would have if she were a fellow soldier on the battlefield. Babbitt was awarded a Purple Heart for the injuries he suffered in Viet Nam. After he was executed, Manny Babbitt received a funeral with military honors.

IV. Hope On The Horizon?

There is an increasing recognition that severe mental illness is a reason to spare people not from responsibility for their crimes, but from the ultimate sanction of death. In 2008, a North Carolina court found that Guy LeGrande was incompetent to be executed. LeGrande appears to be psychotic. During his trial where he represented himself, he wore a Superman shirt and told the jury to "[p]ull the damn switch and shake that groove thing."

Also in 2008, the Governor of Virginia found that Percy Walton was too mentally ill to be executed. Walton thought that after he was executed that he would come back to life. In fact, he believed after his death sentence was carried out, he would go to Burger King to eat hamburgers. He also believed that his dead grandfather and the victims of his crimes would be resurrected.

V. Current Legislation

In 2006, the American Bar Association passed a resolution calling for the exemption of those with serious mental illness from imposition and execution of the death penalty. At the time of this writing, Connecticut is the only state that prohibits the execution of someone who is mentally ill. Connecticut General Statute § 53a-46a (h)(3) (2009) exempts a capital defendant from execution if his "mental capacity was significantly impaired or [his] ability to conform [his] conduct to the requirements of law was significantly impaired but not so impaired in either case as to constitute a defense to prosecution[.]"

Other states legislatures, including Indiana, Kentucky, North Carolina and Tennessee, have proposed bills to exempt capital defendants with severe mental illness from facing the death penalty. This type of legislation is critical to protecting the severely mentally ill from execution. In addition to correcting the fundamental unfairness of capitally trying a person with a severe mental illness, an exemption would also significantly reduce years of expensive and time consuming litigation. If a defendant who is found to suffer from severe mental illness at the trial stage is exempt from the death penalty, the case will proceed as a non-capital one. Because of the necessary additional protections attached to capital cases, the costs of capital trials and appeals is significantly higher for all parties involved—the defense, the prosecution, and the courts. With death off the table for the seriously mentally ill, the costs of the trials and appeals will be significantly reduced in those cases. Most importantly, we will create a criminal justice system that comes closer to ensuring that the punishment fits the crime and the defendant.

> "There are other ways to punish white-collar criminals."

White-Collar Criminals Should Be Given Lighter Sentences

Rob Norton

Rob Norton is a financial consultant and the former economics editor of Fortune *magazine. In the following viewpoint, he argues that the current sentencing guidelines for white-collar criminals are too harsh. Citing numerous results of recent white-collar trials, Norton asserts that politics and public expectations are leading factors in unreasonable punishment for executives who commit fraud and other nonviolent crimes. Although he does not think reform is likely in the near future, he does believe with recent media support changes in these sentencing guidelines are eventually possible.*

As you read, consider the following questions:

1. During what time period has the sentencing of white-collar criminals intensified?

2. How are sentences in financial-fraud cases determined?

Rob Norton, "Let's Reform Those Draconian Sentencing Guidelines," *Corporate Board Member*, January/February 2008. Reproduced by permission. www.boardmember.com.

3. About how many Americans are currently behind bars?

On February 16, 2006, Richard P. Adelson was convicted of securities fraud, deceit, and conspiracy in connection with the overstatement of corporate earnings at Impath, a New York City company that provided diagnostic and laboratory services. Adelson had joined the outfit in 1992 as a salesman and had later become president and chief operating officer, serving until 2003, when an accounting scandal put Impath into bankruptcy—and Adelson in the crosshairs of the U.S. Justice Department. Prosecutors told the court that federal sentencing guidelines called for a prison sentence of 85 years: life without parole.

To many, including *Corporate Board Member*, this seemed excessive. Adelson was a first offender who had led an otherwise blameless, even exemplary, life. More than 100 friends and acquaintances, including clergymen, policemen, and a Harvard dean, attested to his good works and deep humanity. Moreover, he had played a fairly minor role in the fraudulent conduct for which he was convicted. He was penitent, and no one argued that he posed any further danger to society.

Somebody else who was shocked by the prosecution's demand was Jed Rakoff, the U.S. district-court judge who had presided over the case. In a blistering 21-page sentencing memorandum, he wrote that the suggested sentence was "patently unreasonable." Instead Rakoff sentenced Adelson, 40 at the time, to three and a half years in prison and ordered him to pay no less than $50 million in restitution, $1.2 million of which was seized from his forfeited assets, with the rest to be paid out of future income at the rate of 15% per month—meaning he'll most likely be making restitution for the rest of his life. Rakoff also banned Adelson for life from serving as an officer or director of a public company. Prosecutors have appealed the sentence.

Extreme Sentences

The jail time the prosecution sought in Adelson's case was extreme, but it illustrates all too well just how harshly the U.S. criminal justice system approaches corporate fraud cases these days—in part because of an effort to make the penalties for white-collar crime match the draconian punishments imposed in recent decades for even nonviolent street crimes, such as drug possession. But two sentencing wrongs don't make a right.

There are other ways to punish white-collar criminals. As it is, the sentences recently doled out may well mean that some miscreants will die in prison. Former Adelphia CEO John Rigas was 82 when he began his 15-year sentence. Former WorldCom CEO Bernard Ebbers was 63 at the time he was sentenced to 25 years.

Others have been given unusually long sentences as well. Enron CEO Jeffrey Skilling, 52 when his sentence came down, got 24 years; Computer Associates chairman and CEO Sanjay Kumar, 44, got 12 years. They were among those who received federal sentences, for which there is no parole. Tyco International CEO Dennis Kozlowski, then 58, and CFO Mark Swartz, 45, were convicted in a New York State court and given maximum sentences of 25 years. Both will be eligible for parole in eight and one-third years—but they will be serving very hard time. State prison is brutal. . . .

The draconian punishments in the U.S. are a relatively new development in the law. As recently as 20 years ago, white-collar criminals who were first offenders often avoided jail entirely, and rarely served much time. The stiffening of sentences has been especially pronounced in the last 15 years. In 1990, for example, Michael Milken, the most vilified figure in the 1980s "decade of greed" insider-trading scandals, was sentenced to 10 years in jail. The sentence was considered shockingly harsh at the time, but under the rules then in place, Milken would have been eligible for parole in four years. In fact, his sentence was subsequently reduced to two years. Had today's rules been in effect, Milken would probably still be in jail with many more years left to serve—and he'd have a lot of company. In July [2007], the President's Corporate Fraud Task Force, which includes several Justice Department officials and U.S. attorneys plus the heads of eight other federal agencies and departments, announced on its fifth anniversary that it had secured 1,236 convictions, among them those of 214 CEOs and presidents, 53 CFOs, 129 vice presidents, and 23 corporate counsel or attorneys. The list included board insiders, but there is no evidence that outside directors have been jailed or fined for criminal misdeeds. Some, of course, have been sued in civil courts, notably those serving at Enron when the scandal hit; they agreed to pay a combined total of $13 million out of their own pockets to settle a shareholder suit.

One reason the U.S. is a leader in imposing severe prison sentences on white-collar criminals is that American voters want it that way. They have increasingly demanded harsh punishment in general, for both crime in the streets and crime in the suites. Another reason is the increasing eagerness of prosecutors to seek criminal charges in cases that years ago would have been handled in the civil justice systems. That gives them much more formidable tools for prosecuting and convicting white-collar offenders. . . .

Guidelines for Sentencing

In financial-fraud cases, the guidelines get tough by emphasizing the financial loss resulting from a crime. Starting with fraud that produces a loss of up to $5,000, the guidelines set a "base offense level," measured in points, for an instance of fraud, reflecting the defendant's prior criminal record. Then they add points to the offense level as monetary losses rise and other aggravating factors, such as the number of victims, are added.

Thus a first offender guilty of fraud would receive a base offense level of six under the guidelines, which would call for a prison sentence between zero and six months and be left to the judge's discretion. But the points added for financial losses mount quickly and steeply. If a case of fraud results in a loss of more than $1 million, the offense level rises to 22, suggesting a sentence of 41 to 51 months. When losses hit $100 million, the offense level goes to 32, implying a sentence of 10 to 12 years. If an instance of fraud involves more than 250 victims, another six points is added, which pushes the offense level to 38, leading to a sentence of 20 to 25 years.

Anyone accused of fraud at a large public company that results in a big fall in the stock price is therefore at risk of an extremely long prison sentence, almost without exception. In the case of Impath's Richard Adelson, the prosecution argued that the offense level was no less than 55, which Judge Rakoff said was "rather remarkable" considering that the official sentencing table lists only levels from one to 43.

Another factor that pushes up sentences is the government's propensity to layer on additional counts of criminal conduct based on the underlying crime. This is done by adding counts for such things as wire and mail fraud (using a telephone or sending a letter in connection with the base offense) and by applying other statutes, such as the Racketeer Influenced and Corrupt Organizations Act (RICO) and the money-laundering statutes, in cases for which they were clearly not intended.

The Supreme Court ruled in 2007 that the mandatory guidelines were unconstitutional because of another of their controversial features: Congress directed judges to consider "acquitted conduct" in setting sentences. This means that even if a jury acquits the defendant of some charges (using the strict trial definition of guilt beyond a reasonable doubt), the judge is ordered to base the sentence on the acquitted crimes as well if he or she believes the defendant guilty of them (using the much lower standard of "a preponderance of evidence"). The Supreme Court held that taking acquitted conduct into account when sentencing under mandatory guidelines deprived defendants of their right to a trial by jury.

But rather than throwing the guidelines out and asking Congress for wholesale revision, the court, in a pair of fuzzy split decisions, ruled that judges should still use the guidelines as "advisory" and could continue to consider acquitted conduct in sentencing. This past June, in another split decision, the Supreme Court underscored its support for the guidelines and ruled that any sentence falling within the range they set forth should be considered "reasonable" by courts reviewing the sentence on appeal. This also means that any sentence outside the guidelines, such as the one Judge Rakoff imposed on Adelson, can be considered unreasonable and subject to appellate review.

Penalties Go Too Far

Many experts in criminal law feel the multi-decade sentences being handed down today are excessive. "They are absurd, and a waste of time and money," says Roger Williams University's David Zlotnick.

Even some of the prosecutors who helped put Enron officials behind bars believe the penalties that can now be imposed go too far. "We've gotten where we are today without a real discussion," says attorney Samuel Buell, who led the Enron prosecutors' team and now teaches at Washington University Law School in St. Louis. Buell wrote a paper for the *Cardozo Law Review* in 2007, calling for the reform of sentencing for financial-reporting fraud. Asked about some of the recent white-collar crime sentences, he says, "I would say where we're looking at life without parole for white-collar criminal cases, that's absurd."

Some federal judges obviously agree. A few, like Jed Rakoff, have refused to impose the prison sentences called for by

Defining White-Collar Crime

The idea of white-collar crime was first introduced by Edwin H. Sutherland during his presidential address at the American Sociological Society Meeting in 1939. He raised concern over the criminological community's preoccupation with the low status offender and "street crimes" and the relative inattention given to the offenses perpetrated by people in higher status occupations. In his book, *White Collar Crime*, Sutherland explained further that white-collar crime "may be defined approximately as a crime committed by a person of respectability and high social status in the course of his occupation". Unfortunately, this definition seemed to spark more debate rather than further delineate the range of criminal behaviors that constitute white-collar crime. People continue to focus on the word "approximately" and use that as a basis to stretch or shrink the scope of white-collar crime to serve their purposes.

Currently, the definition of white-collar crime is still hotly contested within the community of experts. Although there is a multitude of variations, there appears to be three major orientations: those that define white-collar crime by the type of offender (e.g., high socioeconomic status and/or occupation of trust); those that define it in terms of the type of offense (e.g., economic crime); and those that study it in terms of the organizational culture rather than the offender or offense. Additionally, there are also those that confine the definition mainly to economic crime, as well as others that include other corporate crimes like environmental law violations and health and safety law violations.

Cynthia Barnett, "The Measurement of White-Collar Crime Using Uniform Crime Reporting (UCR) Data," U.S. Department of Justice, Federal Bureau of Investigation, 2002. www.fbi.gov.

the guidelines, daring prosecutors to appeal them. Appellate courts have sent some of those cases back to the judges for harsher sentences, but in other cases the courts have struck down lengthy sentences imposed by judges. For example, Jamie Olis, a midlevel Dynegy executive sentenced in 2004, at age 38, to 24 years for his role in accounting fraud at the energy company, had his sentence reduced to six years on appeal. During its current term, the Supreme Court is considering two cases that could lead to greater clarity about the sentencing guidelines. Both involve district-court sentences that fell short of the guidelines' prescriptions. One defendant who pleaded guilty to being part of an Ecstasy-selling conspiracy when 21 and a college student got probation; another, who admitted to drug offenses involving both powder and crack cocaine, as well as a firearms offense, got 15 years. Circuit courts later sided with prosecutors and ruled the sentences unreasonable, and the Supremes have now heard arguments in the two cases.

Few legal critics hold out much hope for a major change in sentencing patterns anytime soon. One big reason, if not the biggest: politics. The law-and-order movement was originally a Republican Party endeavor for the most part, and many Democrats felt the sentences being given out to minority street criminals were unconscionable. But the [President Bill] Clinton administration made little effort to reform the laws, for fear the party would be seen as soft on crime. Similarly, during George W. Bush's presidency there's been no move to reduce the sentences of white-collar criminals, for fear the Republicans will be seen as beholden to big business. "When push comes to shove," says law professor Douglas Berman, "everyone is inclined to sell out the criminals."

Hope for Reform

One reform that would cut excessive sentences down significantly, of course, would be to prohibit prosecutors from layering additional counts of wire fraud and the like on top of more serious crimes. A more basic reform would be to recognize that the sentencing guidelines that grew out of Americans' late-20th-century fixation on punishment are fundamentally flawed and Congress needs to rewrite them. But that's unlikely, requiring as it would a change in public opinion and, even more improbable, a burst of political leadership. While an established group of public-interest organizations has been lobbying for many years against harsh sentences for minor drug offenders, the business community has been conspicuously absent in lobbying against harsh treatment for white-collar offenders.

Growing awareness of the political and economic consequences of excessive sentencing may yet move public opinion. In recent years, newspapers and magazines have begun noting that the U.S. is now the world leader in both the absolute number and the proportion of its citizens that are in jail. More than two million Americans are behind bars (about the same as the number enrolled in universities). The country's incarceration rate, according to Brown University economics professor Glenn Loury, is 6.2 times that of Canada, 7.8 times that of France, and 12.3 times that of Japan. Loury's primary complaint is with the racial implications of the war on drugs, but he also points out the economic costs. Those are enormous, even though the U.S. corrections sector is big business and accounts for a lot of jobs (and voters)—more, in fact, than the combined workforces of Ford Motor, General Motors, and Wal-Mart, the three largest private-sector employers.

The overarching problem with multi-decade sentences for nonviolent crimes like fraud and drug possession is that they seem disproportionate to the goals prison sentences are supposed to achieve: penitence, deterrence, restitution, and retribution. Does life without parole for a white-collar fraud offender—or 25 years for a single drug offense—really accomplish these things any more effectively than, say, three- to five-year sentences? Perhaps in some specific cases, but surely not in all.

The point was made eloquently by Judge Rakoff in his Adelson sentencing memorandum: "[I]t is obvious that sentencing is the most sensitive, and difficult, task that any judge is called upon to undertake. Where the sentencing guidelines provide reasonable guidance, they are of considerable help to any judge in fashioning a sentence that is fair, just and reasonable. But where, as here, the calculations. . .have so run amok that they are patently absurd on their face, a court is forced to place greater reliance on. . .more general considerations. . .as carefully applied to the particular circumstances of the case and to the human being who will bear the consequences."

| "White-collar crime is already shamefully under-punished."

White-Collar Criminals Should Not Be Released Early

Ming Zhen Shakya

Ming Zhen Shakya is the founder of the Nan Hua Zen Buddhist Society and serves on the board of directors of the Zen Buddhist Order of Hsu Yun. In the following viewpoint, she argues that sentences for violent and nonviolent crimes are often based on class distinctions rather than the severity of the crime. She asserts that wealthy criminals are far less likely to be given strict sentences for their illegal actions, whereas poor criminals are more likely to spend time behind bars. According to Shakya, white-collar criminals should not be released early from prison.

As you read, consider the following questions:

1. What distinction does the author make between violent and nonviolent crimes?

2. How long did it take for the Justice Department to prosecute KKK members for crimes they committed earlier in the century?

Ming Zhen Shakya, "Early Release from Prison: A Bad Idea," *Zen and the Martial Arts*, June 8, 2007. Reproduced by permission of the Zen Buddhist Order of Hsu Yun. http://zatma.org.

3. What was the final decision in the case against Charles Keating?

"Sticks and stones may break my bones, but names will never hurt me." It's a quaint old quip that more and more describes the way we categorize crime. It comes in tandem with that other maxim that illuminates the quality of justice we may all expect: "The Golden Rule states that they who have the gold make the rules."

Violent vs. Non-Violent Crimes

As if we're all afflicted with haphephobia—the fear of being touched—we make peculiar distinctions about violence and non-violence. One man may appropriate the identities of a hundred men and use that information to steal their homes, their assets, and their good names—without committing a single act of violence. But if, as those men pace back and forth, biting their knuckles in despair, one of them so much as shoves that man aside in a show of contempt; ah. . . that man has committed a violent crime.

This division of crime into violent and non-violent has ingrained social implications. Ever since human beings established differences between those who "have" and those who "have not"—regardless of the nature of that which is possessed, be it power, wealth, beauty, and so on—those who have the vaunted commodity seem also to have immunity for their crimes, if not from prosecution, then at least from punishment. Particularly when the class distinction is economic, justice systems—dazzled into benediction by the aura of gold—tend to 'hold harmless' the wealthy and powerful.

It was in feudal times that this perception of an intrinsic difference between refined aristocrats and coarse peasants first informed our definitions of violent crimes (those which involve touching one's person) and non-violent crimes (those which don't). Although rich and poor could certainly commit the same type of crime, different standards applied. Brutish peasants needed rigorously to be controlled lest they raise a hand against their masters. (Even today, without an expressed invitation, protocol prohibits touching royal persons just as bodyguards prevent touching their client.) When nobles killed it was usually considered statecraft or sport. Jurisprudence had its positive side: nothing could keep a noble more fit or more discreet than Trial By Combat, a frequent method of determining the winner's innocence.

How ingrained this sense of inferiority was can be seen in the strange fact that what was violent and punishable when committed by peasants was often the benign privilege of aristocracy. Rape, amongst peasants, was a crime; but the act had a different character when nobility was involved. Under the law of *Jus primae noctis* or *Droit du seigneur*, feudal lords had the right to deflower a peasant's bride. Whether she liked it or not, the bride's wedding night was spent with the lord of the manor, not with her husband. And while a nobleman could hardly be charged with raping a peasant, a peasant's raping of a noblewoman—if he were sufficiently demented to attempt it—would be met with an unpleasant execution.

In ways gross or subtle, property crimes revealed the strange distinctions in class justice. Illiterate peasants did not own property, they *were* property. They could pilfer, filch, snatch, pinch or swipe from each other; but, as the verbs suggest, these were trifling crimes, adjudicated by priests or constables. For violent crimes—such as taking the nobles' property by killing a deer or another peasant, nobles could preside at the trial.

But only the literate aristocracy could commit serious property crimes in which written instruments determined ownership: larceny, fraud, embezzlement, forgery; and only nobles could judge each other. It was unthinkable that the common man could ever sit in judgment of the aristocracy; and not even centuries of legislative equality and the power to sit on a jury of his "peers" has ever dispelled the notion that somehow the ordinary man is not quite qualified to judge his economic superiors.

Bias Remains

And it is still unfortunately true that the seriousness of a crime depends more on the status of the persons involved than it does with the act, itself. When a society deems certain people intrinsically inferior and crimes are committed against them, reason's will to rectify the injustice has to grapple with that ingrained sense of holding harmless the superior person, i.e., the one who did the harming. (When the KKK murdered black citizens fifty years ago, it took the Justice Department more than a generation to hold anyone responsible. Old KKK defendants needed walkers and oxygen to make it into court. When 50 prostitutes were killed and dumped into the Green River in Washington State over a period of nearly 20 years, it took the police that long to charge Gary Ridgway with the crime—and then they let him plea bargain his way out of the death penalty.)

While the various justice systems show no reluctance to punish the poor, they all seem to retain that innate renitence to discomfit the rich. In a landscape filled with video cameras to catch a furtive shoplifter, the magnitude and the duration of corporate criminal activity and the brazenness with which fraudulently obtained money is squandered—for example, a $2 million birthday party given by a CEO for his wife; all attest to this peculiar double standard. Our various regulatory agencies are more blind than Justice aspires to be. Anyone who doubts this should consider WorldCom; Enron; Adelphia; Quest; Tyco; the list is endless. Perhaps the best example of the judicial generosity shown to a rich person whose "errors" caused him the inconvenience of arrest is the case of Charles Keating of the great Savings and Loan debacle.

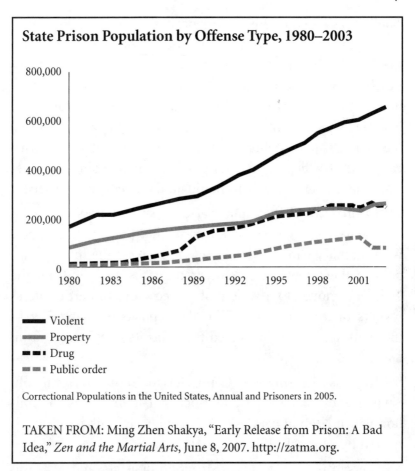

State Prison Population by Offense Type, 1980–2003

- ▬ Violent
- ▬ Property
- ▬ ▪ Drug
- ▪ ▪ ▪ Public order

Correctional Populations in the United States, Annual and Prisoners in 2005.

TAKEN FROM: Ming Zhen Shakya, "Early Release from Prison: A Bad Idea," *Zen and the Martial Arts*, June 8, 2007. http://zatma.org.

The Savings and Loan Debacle

In 1980, Keating's American Continental Corporation (ACC), a real estate investment company, began to invest in Phoenix, Arizona's booming real estate market. At this time, the savings and loan [S & L] institutions were in deep financial trouble. In the [Jimmy] Carter administration, the Fed [Federal Reserve], in a move to stem inflation, had drastically raised interest rates; and the S & Ls, unable by law to increase the low rate of interest they paid on deposits, faced bankruptcy as their customers withdrew their accounts to place them in banks in which they'd earn three times as much in interest.

The S & Ls had lent out their depositors' money on low interest 30 year mortgages. Now, as the depositors withdrew funds, the S & Ls were unable to meet the withdrawal requests without borrowing money. By law, also, they were narrowly limited to the kinds of loans they could make, a restraint which hampered their ability to compete in more lucrative markets. S & L assets quickly slipped away as they approached the critical point at which the federal government was obliged to declare them insolvent and to liquidate their remaining assets.

In order to avert a financial disaster, Congress moved to deregulate the Savings and Loans so that they could compete with ordinary banks by being able to increase the interest they paid to their depositors; issue credit cards; borrow from the Fed; lend money to a variety of projects and to participate as owners in those projects. To make deposits with the S & Ls more attractive, they increased the deposits they insured from $40,000 to $100,000.

In 1984, Keating's ACC purchased California's Lincoln Savings and Loan and its 30 branches. The price was $55 million which Keating paid using $51 million in junk bonds engineered by Michael Milken.

Lincoln's life's blood was $1 billion in assets; and ACC was in desperate need of a transfusion. Keating moved Lincoln's main office to Phoenix, installed his cronies in administrative positions, and proceeded to bleed Lincoln dry.

Using Lincoln's money, ACC purchased 20,000 acres of land southwest of Phoenix for an average $3,000 an acre ($60 million). The plan was to develop the land, now called Estrella Mountain Ranch, until, by the year 2000 it would contain 50,000 custom homes, the individual lots of which would be worth an exponentially greater sum than the *original* cost. By 1987 Lincoln had invested $100 million originally in the development. ACC was building office buildings and hotels—including the grandiose $300 million Phoenician Hotel that had everything but guests. On the surface, Keating appeared to epitomize the American Tycoon: private jet, helicopter, the works.

The "Grand Illusion"

As the government would later charge, ACC's success was a grand illusion. ACC sold parcels of Estrella land at extremely inflated prices to "straw buyers" who borrowed money from Lincoln to pay ACC for the land that Lincoln had furnished ACC with the money to buy. ACC made $82 million in "profit" which enabled Keating and his associates to receive huge salaries and bonuses and to make productive contributions to the campaigns of five U.S. Senators.

Keating now offered his admirers the opportunity to buy $250 million of ACC bonds. Naturally, he could not have the bonds underwritten—that would mean that ACC would have to be audited. Keating quietly skipped that nicety, and the undesirable bonds were marketed by the only financial institution that would touch them—his own Lincoln S & L. Misled by salesmen into believing that the bonds were federally insured, 23,000 ordinary folks, many who trusted Keating with their life savings, bought the $250 million load of fancy paper. Worse, the bonds were subordinated debentures and could be paid off only after ACC paid off its other debts.

In 1989 ACC suddenly declared bankruptcy and within twenty-four hours federal agents seized control of Lincoln S & L. The numbers added up to $3.2 billion, the costliest S & L failure in U.S. history. American taxpayers had to cough up $2 billion to cover Lincoln's insured losses. If Keating's business practices were not sleazy enough—and they certainly ought to have been—days before he declared bankruptcy, he looted ACC of its final million dollars.

Keating was charged in both federal and state (California) court with fraud, racketeering, and conspiracy. Called to testify before the Senate Banking Committee, he took the 5th [refused to testify by claiming protection against self-incrimination under the Fifth Amendment].

Lance Ito presided over Keating's California trial with the same degree of incompetence he displayed when he presided over the O.J. Simpson [murder] trial [in 1995]. Keating, a practicing Catholic, had donated $1.25 million to Mother Teresa in India in time for her to oblige him by writing a personal letter to Judge Ito telling him what a good man Keating was. Despite this saintly testament, Keating was convicted of all charges and sentenced to ten years in prison; but the appellate court overturned his conviction because Judge Ito had somehow forgotten to instruct the jury that "intent" mattered.

Keating was also convicted in federal court, receiving a sentence of twelve years. But this conviction, too, miraculously was overturned on grounds that it was possible that some of the federal jurors had been influenced by the decision of the California jurors.

He was granted a new federal trial; but he avoided that by reaching a plea agreement: he admitted to bankruptcy fraud committed when he looted ACC of that final million, and the federal prosecutors dropped all charges against him and his family. He was sentenced to time served—the four years he had been in jail pending his appeals.

A federal class action suit filed by those he had defrauded resulted in a $3.3 billion judgment against him. It was later reduced to $1.6 billion (mere peanuts to the bankrupt).

The Securities and Exchange Commission filed and won its case against Keating which was settled in 1994 when Keating, already bankrupt, promised to repay millions of dollars if he ever found enough money.

The government's Resolution Trust Corporation that officially took over Lincoln when it was declared insolvent filed another case against Keating. The result in 1994 was a summary judgment of $4.3 billion against Keating and his wife. In 1999, the decision was overturned on appeal.

The U.S. Supreme Court was asked to rule on the Appellate Court's decision to overturn Keating's conviction in Lance Ito's court. They refused to hear the appeal in October 2000. State prosecutors declined to request a new trial.

Releasing Non-Violent Offenders

The rippling effect of this catastrophic non-violent crime brought suffering to so many decent citizens. If Keating had mugged only one of them, he would likely have served more time. It is safe to say that despite the frailty of many of the elderly, if they were asked to choose either the physical pain of being the victim of assault and battery or the anguish and hardship caused by the loss of their savings, there would be blood on the streets but no regrets about it.

And now we have another opportunity for conscience to compromise itself. States, confronted with the problem of overcrowded prisons, have chosen to solve the problem by reducing prison populations! Even before "non-violent" inmates are eligible to apply for parole, they are being released. To bureaucrats and swindlers this must sound like a splendid idea. Many of us are shaking our heads in disbelief.

Which crimes are considered violent and which are not? Here is a selection from the U.S. Department of Justice's September 6, 2006 list (www.ojp.usdoj.gov/bjs):

Violent offenses include the usual "touching" crimes of murder, manslaughter, rape, sexual assault, assault, intimidation, criminal endangerment, and so on.

Crimes that are serious but not categorized as violent are property offenses such as burglary, larceny, car theft, fraud, possession and selling of stolen property, destruction of property, trespassing, vandalism, criminal tampering, and so on. Drug offenses include possessing, making, and trafficking. Public-order offenses include drunk driving, and a variety of vice crimes.

Such crimes as identity and credit card theft; embezzlement; forgery; corporation racketeering, "confidence" scams, Internet deceptions, and all manner of financial misrepresentations are considered non-violent. After the public has paid by being victimized by these criminals, and then for their apprehension and trial, state legislators are now saving money by setting them free. And it is public safety, we are told, that is the primary consideration in the early release program.

White-collar crime is already shamefully under-punished. That the states would prefer to release people who belong in prison when there are so many drug addicts and mentally ill inmates who do not—makes little or no sense. . . .

But worst of all, the poor have the additional burden of knowing that Justice, far from being blind, carefully separates the rich, the powerful, the celebrated—and applies to them a different and far more lenient standard.

Periodical Bibliography

The following articles have been selected to supplement the diverse views presented in this chapter.

Sasha Abramsky   "A Worthy Diversion," *American Prospect*, July/August 2008.

Michael Friscolanti   "Predators Still Loose," *Maclean's*, January 19, 2008.

Sarah Hammond   "Adults or Kids?" *State Legislatures*, April 2008.

Mark Ivory   "Why Are They in Prison?" *Community Care*, March 5, 2009.

Gara LaMarche   "After Willie Horton," *Nation*, June 25, 2007.

Laurel Maury   "It's Too Late for Me," *Progressive*, September 2008.

Mark Nolan   "Pleading Insanity and Mental State Defenses," *Legaldate*, July 2008.

Matthew L. Perdoni,   "Addressing the Treatment Needs of Jail
Faye S. Taxman, and   Inmates: Missing Public Health and Safety
Bennett W. Fletcher   Opportunities," *American Jails*, May/June 2008.

David Scharf   "Are Day Reporting and Reentry Programs the Future of Corrections in Our Country?" *American Jails*, July/August 2008.

Emma Schwartz   "A Chance for Justice at Last," *U.S. News & World Report*, February 25, 2008.

Mark T. Simpson   "Identifying the Proper Drug-Abuse Treatment for Offenders," *Corrections Today*, December 2008.

Scott VanBenschoten   "Risk/Needs Assessment: Is This the Best We Can Do?" *Federal Probation*, September 2008.

How Can Crime Be Prevented?

Chapter Preface

The twentieth century was marked by a series of shootings that kept gun control laws at the forefront of most political campaigns. Beginning with the fatal shooting of President John F. Kennedy in 1963 to the mass killing by two students at Columbine High School [Littleton, Colorado] in 1999, Americans have considered and reconsidered the right of civilians to bear arms. That right has been preserved largely because few studies show that the abolition of private gun ownership will reduce the overall crime rate. Instead, concerned citizens have been fighting for stricter regulations for gun ownership, but some supporters of gun ownership wonder if more laws are worth the cost to personal liberty.

On February 24, 1994, the Brady Bill was passed into law. Named after James Brady, who was shot and paralyzed in the attempted assassination of President Ronald Reagan in 1981, it requires that all gun purchasers pass a federal background check, which can take up to three days to complete. It is believed that if guns can be kept out of the hands of potentially dangerous persons, such as former felons, then citizens will be safer without completely restricting gun ownership. "Saving Lives by Taking Guns Out of Crime," a study released in 2000 by the Center to Prevent Handgun Violence, reveals that in the first five years after the Brady Bill was passed more than nine thousand lives were saved because it limited dangerous criminals' access to firearms. Dr. Douglas Weil, director of research for the Center, reasons that "by preventing gun sales to felons and other prohibited purchasers and by disrupting the movement of illegal guns across state lines, the Brady Law reduces criminal gun use."

Opponents of tougher gun laws argue that stricter regulations will not prevent gun crimes, but will put guns into the hands of more criminals instead. According to the Bureau of

Alcohol, Tobacco, and Firearms (BATF) in 2003, 93 percent of the guns used in crimes were not obtained through lawful purchase. Therefore, waiting periods and other restrictions will not likely deter the majority of criminals from obtaining and using a firearm to commit a crime. The CATO Institute reports the 2001 findings of Florida State University professor Gary Kleck, who found that waiting periods had no statistically significant affect on reducing firearm-related crimes. In addition, proponents of the Second Amendment argue that gun ownership can be life saving. John Barnes, analyst at the Washington Policy Center, cites statistics in May 2006 that show "at least 2.5 million protective uses of guns each year in the U.S. Guns are used about three to five times as often for defensive purposes as for criminal purposes."

In the end, most people agree that having laws concerning firearm ownership are necessary. The strictness of those laws and how they are enforced remain up for debate. As the authors in this chapter demonstrate, determining the best way to prevent crime is not an easy task. The rights of all of those involved make the issue far more complicated than either side is willing to admit.

| "Capital punishment produces a strong
deterrent effect that saves lives."

The Death Penalty
Deters Crime

David B. Muhlhausen

In the following viewpoint, David B. Muhlhausen, senior policy analyst in the Center for Data Analysis at The Heritage Foundation, presents his views on the death penalty to the Subcommittee on the Constitution, Civil Rights, and Property Rights of the Committee on the Judiciary of the United States Senate. He uses the findings of several studies to prove that in states where the death penalty is an option for punishment, crime rates have decreased. In addition, he disputes claims of racial discrimination in capital punishment cases and points to recent surveys that show that most Americans support executing violent criminals.

As you read, consider the following questions:

1. What are the main principles of deterrence theory?

2. What are the three main findings of Professor Joanna M. Shepherd's research?

David B. Muhlhausen, "The Death Penalty Deters Crime and Saves Lives," U.S. Senate Committee on the Judiciary, June 27, 2007. Reproduced by permission of The Heritage Foundation. http://judiciary.senate.gov.

3. According to the studies discussed by the author, about how many murders does each execution prevent?

While opponents of capital punishment have been very vocal in their opposition, Gallup opinion polls consistently demonstrate that the American public overwhelmingly supports capital punishment. In Gallup's most recent poll, 67 percent of Americans favor the death penalty for those convicted of murder, while only 28 percent are opposed. From 2000 to the most recent poll in 2006, support for capital punishment consistently runs a 2:1 ratio in favor.

Despite strong public support for capital punishment, federal, state, and local officials must continually ensure that its implementation rigorously upholds constitutional protections, such as due process and equal protection of the law. However, the criminal process should not be abused to prevent the lawful imposition of the death penalty in appropriate capital cases.

Alleged Racial Discrimination

As of December 2005, there were 37 prisoners under a sentence of death in the federal system. Of these prisoners, 43.2 percent were white, while 54.1 percent were African American. The fact that African Americans are a majority of federal prisoners on death row and a minority in the overall United States population may lead some to conclude that the federal system discriminates against African Americans. However, there is little rigorous evidence that such disparities exist in the federal system.

Under a competitive grant process, the National Institute of Justice awarded the RAND Corporation a grant to determine whether racial disparities exist in the federal death penalty system. The resulting 2006 RAND study set out to determine what factors, including the defendant's race, victim's race, and crime characteristics, affect the decision to seek a death penalty case. Three independent teams of researchers were tasked with developing their own methodologies to analyze the data. Only after each team independently drew their own conclusions did they share their findings with each other.

When first looking at the raw data without controlling for case characteristics, RAND found that large race effects with the decision to seek the death penalty are more likely to occur when the defendants are white and when the victims are white. However, these disparities disappeared in each of the three studies when the heinousness of the crimes was taken into account. The RAND study concludes that the findings support the view that decisions to seek the death penalty are driven by characteristics of crimes rather than by race. RAND's findings are very compelling because three independent research teams, using the same data but different methodologies, reached the same conclusions.

While there is little evidence that the federal capital punishment system treats minorities unfairly, some may argue that the death penalty systems in certain states may be discriminatory. One such state is Maryland. In May 2001, then-Governor Parris Glendening instituted a moratorium on the use of capital punishment in Maryland in light of concerns that it may be unevenly applied to minorities, especially African Americans. In 2000, Governor Glendening commissioned University of Maryland Professor of Criminology Ray Paternoster to study the possibility of racial discrimination in the application of the death penalty in Maryland. The results of Professor Paternoster's study found that black defendants who murder white victims are substantially more likely to be charged with a capital crime and sentenced to death.

In 2003, Governor Robert L. Ehrlich wisely lifted the moratorium. His decision was justified. In 2005, a careful review of the study by Professor of Statistics and Sociology Richard Berk of the University of California, Los Angeles, and his co-authors found that the results of Professor Paternoster's study do not stand up to statistical scrutiny. According to Professor Berk's re-analysis, "For both capital charges and death sentences, race either played no role or a small role that is very difficult to specify. In short, it is very difficult to find convincing evidence for racial effects in the Maryland data and if there are any, they may not be additive." Further, race may have a small influence because "cases with a black defendant and white victim or 'other' racial combination are *less* likely to have a death sentence."

The Deterrent Effect of the Death Penalty

Federal, state, and local officials need to recognize that the death penalty saves lives. How capital punishment affects murder rates can be explained through general deterrence theory, which supposes that increasing the risk of apprehension and punishment for crime deters individuals from committing crime. Nobel laureate Gary S. Becker's seminal 1968 study of the economics of crime assumed that individuals respond to the costs and benefits of committing crime.

According to deterrence theory, criminals are no different from law-abiding people. Criminals "rationally maximize their own self-interest (utility) subject to constraints (prices, incomes) that they face in the marketplace and elsewhere." Individuals make their decisions based on the net costs and benefits of each alternative. Thus, deterrence theory provides a basis for analyzing how capital punishment should influence murder rates. Over the years, several studies have demonstrated a link between executions and decreases in murder rates. In fact, studies done in recent years, using sophisticated panel data methods, consistently demonstrate a strong link between executions and reduced murder incidents.

The rigorous examination of the deterrent effect of capital punishment began with research in the 1970s by Isaac Ehrlich, currently a University of Buffalo Distinguished Professor of Economics. Professor Ehrlich's research found that the death penalty had a strong deterrent effect. While his research was debated by other scholars, additional research by Professor Ehrlich reconfirmed his original findings. In addition, research by Professor Stephen K. Layson of the University of North Carolina at Greensboro strongly reconfirmed Ehrlich's previous findings.

Numerous studies published over the past few years, using panel data sets and sophisticated social science techniques, are demonstrating that the death penalty saves lives. Panel studies observe multiple units over several periods. The addition of multiple data collection points gives the results of capital punishment panel studies substantially more credibility than the results of studies that have only single before-and-after intervention measures. Further, the longitudinal nature of the panel data allows researchers to analyze the impact of the death penalty over time that cross-sectional data sets cannot address.

Lowering the Murder Rate

Using a panel data set of over 3,000 counties from 1977 to 1996, Professors Hashem Dezhbakhsh, Paul R. Rubin, and Joanna M. Shepherd of Emory University found that each execution, on average, results in 18 fewer murders. Using state-level panel data from 1960 to 2000, Professors Dezhbakhsh and Shepherd were able to compare the relationship between executions and murder incidents before, during, and after the U.S. Supreme Court's death penalty moratorium. They found that executions had a highly significant negative relationship with murder incidents. Additionally, the implementation of state moratoria is associated with the increased incidence of murders.

Separately, Professor Shepherd's analysis of monthly data from 1977 to 1999 found three important findings.

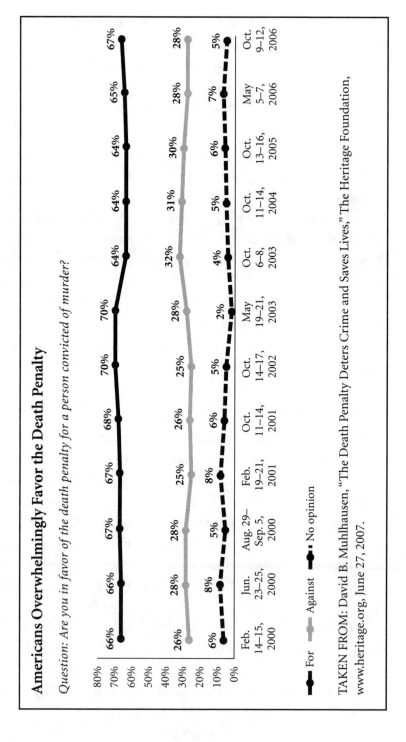

Americans Overwhelmingly Favor the Death Penalty

Question: Are you in favor of the death penalty for a person convicted of murder?

TAKEN FROM: David B. Muhlhausen, "The Death Penalty Deters Crime and Saves Lives," The Heritage Foundation, www.heritage.org, June 27, 2007.

First, each execution, on average, is associated with three fewer murders. The deterred murders included both crimes of passion and murders by intimates.

Second, executions deter the murder of whites and African Americans. Each execution prevents the murder of one white person, 1.5 African Americans, and 0.5 persons of other races.

Third, shorter waits on death row are associated with increased deterrence. For each additional 2.75-year reduction in the death row wait until execution, one murder is deterred.

Professors H. Naci Mocan and R. Kaj Gittings of the University of Colorado at Denver have published two studies confirming the deterrent effect of capital punishment. The first study used state-level data from 1977 to 1997 to analyze the influence of executions, commutations, and removals from death row on the incidence of murder. For each additional execution, on average, about five murders were deterred. Alternatively, for each additional commutation, on average, five additional murders resulted. A removal from death row by either state courts or the U.S. Supreme Court is associated with an increase of one additional murder. Addressing criticism of their work, Professors Mocan and Gittings conducted additional analyses and found that their original findings provided robust support for the deterrent effect of capital punishment.

Two studies by Paul R. Zimmerman, a Federal Communications Commission economist, also support the deterrent effect of capital punishment. Using state-level data from 1978 to 1997, Zimmerman found that each additional execution, on average, results in 14 fewer murders. Zimmerman's second study, using similar data, found that executions conducted by electrocution are the most effective at providing deterrence.

Using a small state-level data set from 1995 to 1999, Professor Robert B. Ekelund of Auburn University and his colleagues analyzed the effect that executions have on single incidents of murder and multiple incidents of murder. They found that executions reduced single murder rates, while there was no effect on multiple murder rates.

Capital Punishment Saves Lives

In summary, the recent studies using panel data techniques have confirmed what we learned decades ago: Capital punishment does, in fact, save lives. Each additional execution appears to deter between three and 18 murders. While opponents of capital punishment allege that it is unfairly used against African Americans, each additional execution deters the murder of 1.5 African Americans. Further moratoria, commuted sentences, and death row removals appear to increase the incidence of murder.

The strength of these findings has caused some legal scholars, originally opposed to the death penalty on moral grounds, to rethink their case. In particular, Professor Cass R. Sunstein of the University of Chicago has commented:

> If the recent evidence of deterrence is shown to be correct, then opponents of capital punishment will face an uphill struggle on moral grounds. If each execution is saving lives, the harms of capital punishment would have to be very great to justify its abolition, far greater than most critics have heretofore alleged.

Americans support capital punishment for two good reasons. First, there is little evidence to suggest that minorities are treated unfairly. Second, capital punishment produces a strong deterrent effect that saves lives.

| "The promise of fairness, deterrence, closure and finality do not ring true."

The Death Penalty Does Not Deter Crime

Aundré M. Herron

Aundré M. Herron is on the board of directors of Death Penalty Focus, a nonprofit organization dedicated to the abolishment of the death penalty. In the following viewpoint, she argues that the death penalty does not deter crime, and it does not bring closure to victims of violent crimes. Following the murder of her brother, she understood the impulse that some victims feel to kill perpetrators. She, however, quickly realized that putting to death the men who murdered her brother would not bring closure to her or her family. Herron believes capital punishment is a waste of valuable resources.

As you read, consider the following questions:

1. What two main professional positions did the author hold that affected her understanding of the death penalty?

2. According to the author, how many people on death row have been exonerated?

Aundré M. Herron, "The Death Penalty Is Not Civilized," *The Sacramento Bee*, April 20, 2008. Reproduced by permission. www.sacbee.com.

3. From 1991 to 2008, how many people were executed in the state of California?

I am no stranger to murder. Not that I have ever killed anyone, but I have lost several members of my family to homicide. What makes me different from most people who share my experience is that I have worked as a lawyer on both sides of the criminal justice system.

I began my career as a district attorney. I filed criminal charges that made defendants eligible for execution and, through trials or pleas, put people in jail for everything from bad checks to murder. I was just doing my job, almost oblivious to the gravity of the role I played. In 1991, I went to "the other side" and began doing appeals for California prisoners sentenced to death, fighting against the very system I once served. But nothing prepared me for the challenge I soon had to face in my own life.

Executions Do Not Bring Closure

In 1994, three years into my work on behalf of people sentenced to die for murder, my brother, Danny "Deuce," was killed in Kansas City, [Missouri]. He was a decorated Vietnam veteran who, after the war, found employment as a redcap at Amtrak. Eventually, he worked his way up to engineer and commanded the route from Chicago to Los Angeles. I couldn't believe my big brother actually "drove" the train. He was an amazing guy and a fantastic big brother. His murder was a devastating blow to my family and to everyone who knew him.

Even though I was working as a death penalty defense lawyer at the time, I was shocked at my impulse to hunt down and kill the perpetrators myself. Eventually, they were caught, but legal technicalities led to dismissal of the case. The cold, cruel reality I had to face was that no one was going to be held responsible for my brother's murder. But even if the case could have gone forward, nothing could replace what my family had lost. Nothing—not the death penalty, not the worst punishment I could imagine for his killers—would ever bring him back. There was no "closure" to be had.

Having served on both sides of the criminal justice system, the experience of losing my brother in this unforgettably tragic way, without recourse or retribution, forced me to re-examine the way "execution" and "closure" are joined in contrived alliance, recited by death penalty advocates to justify their point of view. But having survived my brother's murder without the "benefit" of the death penalty, it is clear to me that the death penalty cannot do what its proponents claim.

It does not deter crime. It is not administered fairly or equitably. It does not bring closure. Instead, it forever ties the victim's survivors and the entire society to the act of ritualistic revenge killing. It is costing us a fortune—fiscally and spiritually. It stands in the way of our ability to live up to our highest ideals regarding justice and the sanctity of life. It is one of our most colossal public-policy failures and should be abolished without delay.

Abolishing the Death Penalty

Abolishing the death penalty isn't about "pro" or "con" partisanship, it's about priorities. And any fair assessment of what our priorities ought to be cannot rationally include the death penalty. We can protect the public without the death penalty. We can punish those who take innocent lives without ourselves engaging in the business of killing.

We cannot trust death penalty proponents who glibly assure us that police, prosecutors and the state are infallible and have never lied or made a mistake. Nor should we entrust power to those who tell us that mistakes are inevitable. We will never know how many innocent people we have executed,

Death Penalty Facts

When touting superficially powerful arguments in favor of the state executing our fellow human beings, the media and academics have a duty to acknowledge the facts contradicting their claims. . . .

- Murder rates are lower in states without the death penalty. This holds true even when comparing neighboring states.

- While Southern states account for over 80 percent of the executions in this country, they have consistently had the highest murder rate of the nation's four regions.

- Since 1972, homicide rates in Canada and the United States have moved in lockstep, yet in that period, Canada has not executed a single person and the United States has executed over 1,000 people. When homicides go down in the United States, they go down in Canada, even though Canada does not use capital punishment.

Jeremy J. Collins,
"Death Penalty No Deterrent to Murder,"
The Carrboro Citizen, July 19, 2007.

but we can put an end to the mistakes like the ones that have been exposed by 128 exonerations of people from death rows across the country.

We can sentence people to die in prison, what we call "life without parole." It prevents those who have committed heinous crimes from re-offending society. The thought of living out one's natural life behind bars is a far worse punishment than execution, with greater potential to deter those who might take a life.

Over the last 17 years, the state [of California] has executed 13 people, some of whom were laudable candidates for clemency, some of whom likely were innocent of the crimes for which they were sentenced to die. These executions did not make us safer, nor has the lack of executions made us less safe. Thankfully, California has not executed anyone in the past two years [2006–2008].

Rejecting State-Sanctioned Killing

Californians must demand a higher standard of themselves and of their leaders. We must reject state-sanctioned killing. We must reject revenge as public policy. We must reject a criminal justice scheme that systematically targets the poor, the mentally ill, the disenfranchised and the dispossessed. We can ensure public safety by investing our resources and our intelligence in front-end solutions to the problem of violent crime.

The smart money would be on an intelligent, humane, more progressive approach to fighting crime and on helping all citizens live quality lives. It is time to send a strong message to the governor and to politicians throughout the state and across this nation that we are weary of the ineffective, cost-prohibitive, unjust and failed death penalty experiment.

The promises of fairness, deterrence, closure and finality do not ring true. We need leaders who inspire solutions, not hatred and fear. We need leaders who can think, not politicians who seek our votes based on their willingness to put people to death.

We must demand that our public resources be put to a higher purpose. We must use our intelligence to attack the problem of violent crime at its source—where the demons of dysfunction, deprivation and denial of opportunity converge to set our children on a path to violent crime rather than a path to becoming community leaders. We must adopt a system that removes the offenders from society without engaging in ritualistic, deliberate, premeditated, cold-blooded acts of state-sanctioned killing carried out at the stroke of midnight and given the false imprimatur of justice.

We are better than that, and we can do better than this.

I *"Newark does appear to be getting safer."*

Surveillance Equipment Helps Reduce Crime

Spencer E. Ante

Spencer E. Ante is the computers department editor for Business Week *from which the following viewpoint is excerpted. He discusses the recent success of the use of surveillance equipment by the police department in Newark, New Jersey. City officials are hoping that the reduction in crime will not only make the city safer for residents, but also will encourage businesses to move into the downtown district, which is only ten miles away from New York City. Ante argues that although Newark's crime-fighting experiment remains in its infancy stage, the initial findings prove promising for the implementation of surveillance equipment in other large U.S. cities.*

As you read, consider the following questions:

1. By what percentage has the murder rate in Newark improved since the implementation of surveillance equipment?

2. Where are most of the surveillance cameras in Newark installed?

Spencer E. Ante, "Newark and the Future of Crime Fighting," *Business Week*, August 25, 2008. Copyright © 2008 by McGraw-Hill, Inc. Reproduced by permission.

3. What event prompted Newark's new administration to begin using surveillance equipment to police its streets?

One recent spring day, two cops in the Newark [New Jersey] Police Dept. watched a shoot-out erupt in broad daylight. Two suspected drug dealers started blasting away at each other in the middle of an apartment complex. The cops didn't witness the violence on the beat, though. They watched it from the city's new communications command center, which collects live video feeds from more than 100 surveillance cameras scattered across the crime-ridden city.

As the shooting broke out, the policemen zoomed in on the scene with a joystick controller. They saw one gunman flee, while the other dragged himself into a nearby apartment, one blood-soaked leg trailing behind. Because of the camera network, the Newark police were able to dispatch a team to the crime scene immediately—90 seconds before the first 911 calls. The gunman who crawled into his apartment was arrested on the spot. "Those complexes are like mazes, but we knew exactly where to send the unit," says Sergeant Marvin Carpenter, commanding officer of the communications post.

The surveillance system is the centerpiece of Mayor Cory Booker's ambitious plan to use cutting-edge technologies to slash Newark's violent crime rate. This August [2008], Newark finished its initial deployment of 111 cameras, adding 76 to the 35 that were in place last summer [2007]. Newark is investing in a whole range of tools, everything from mundane PCs to more novel technologies such as a new citywide broadband wireless network that will let cops fill out police reports from their squad cars instead of schlepping back to the station house. By late fall, Newark expects to complete the deployment of an audio sensor system to pinpoint gunshot locations that cameras fail to catch. "We are trying to leave *The Flintstones* and get to *The Jetsons*," says Booker.

Major cities such as London, New York, and Chicago have rolled out larger video surveillance networks. But technology

Video Surveillance Works in North Dallas

Richland Park Estates is an area in North Dallas that got national attention two years ago [2006] when it became one of the first middle-class neighborhoods in the country to subject itself to 24-hour video surveillance. I drove through there a few weeks ago to see how they were doing. . . .

I look around for cameras, of course, but they are concealed. Eventually I find my way to the meticulously kept home of Dick Becker, former president of the homeowners' association, who shows me the books he keeps on neighborhood crime.

Using data from the police department, Becker has built Excel files showing crime within Richland Park dropping from high rates to almost zero since the cameras were installed two years ago.

"To give you some idea," Becker says, "just in our homeowners' association area in the last 100 weeks there have been 28 incidents. In the previous 12 weeks before cameras, we had 27 incidents."

Jim Schutze, "Are Surveillance Cameras the Answer to Rising East Dallas Crime Rates?" Dallas Observer, *March 6, 2008. www.dallasobserver.com.*

experts say Newark, New Jersey's largest city, is the first metropolis to combine an array of technologies on a large scale. "I haven't seen a city with this mix of technology all in one place," says Kevin Kilgore, president of Let's Think Wireless, a New York company that has built wireless networks for several hundred cities, including Newark.

Bangalore Across the Hudson

With a nod to New York City's revival, Booker is betting that crime reduction will trigger the economic rebirth of Newark, a city of about 280,000 with a proud industrial history that has never fully recovered from the upheavals of the 1960s. In a slowing economy, the charismatic 39-year-old, a Rhodes Scholar and graduate of Yale University Law School, is pitching Newark as a sort of Bangalore across the Hudson: a low-cost place to do business 10 miles from Manhattan, with the second busiest U.S. port, many transportation hubs, sports arenas, and a cluster of schools such as Rutgers University and Seton Hall University School of Law. "You can work your tail off on economic development, but businesses won't come if it's not safe," says Hans Dekker, president of the Newark Community Foundation.

Newark is also a test bed for the tensions between surveillance and privacy. Privacy advocates have raised concerns over the aggressive rollout of video cameras, audio sensors, and other technologies. Critics argue that such surveillance is susceptible to abuse, can have a chilling effect on public life, and hasn't been proven to reduce crime. "The costs are high, and the benefits in terms of law enforcement are low," says Deborah Jacobs, executive director of the New Jersey chapter of the American Civil Liberties Union (ACLU). Whether Newark can strike an acceptable balance between crime-fighting and privacy may determine whether other cities follow similar strategies in the future.

Already though, the business community is beginning to throw its weight behind Booker's plan. In August [2008], Newark scored a big win when London-based Standard Chartered Bank opened a new office downtown that will hold more than 500 employees. Inspired by the mayor's vision, financial executives, such as New York hedge fund operator William Ackman, have financed some of the new technologies that the city can't afford because of its $180 million budget deficit. And the Newark offices of big companies such as Verizon Communications, AT&T, Cablevision Systems, Public Service Enterprise Group, and Continental Airlines are beginning to hire more residents from the city.

Audible.com, a subsidiary of Amazon.com, is one of the companies that has jumped on the mayor's bandwagon. Last March [2007] the company moved its headquarters and 165 employees out of Wayne, [New Jersey], and into a 50,000-square-foot office in downtown Newark. Don Katz, Audible.com's founder and CEO, says the space is 50% cheaper than Manhattan real estate. And even though Katz expected Newark's reputation to scare away some employees, not one worker has left since the move. "For a long time, I thought it would be great if we could serve our shareholders and be part of an urban renaissance," says Katz. "All in all, it's been a complete win."

Improved Police Strategy

Newark does appear to be getting safer, though many areas outside the downtown district remain dangerous. This year [2008] there have been 37 murders, down 40% from 62 in the same period a year ago [2007]. Shooting incidents are down 19%. Over the last year, 101 arrests were made based on live or recorded video evidence. Police officials say the surveillance technology has helped but also stress the effort is one part of the police department's overall strategy. The department, for instance, has created a narcotics squad and added 159 cops since 2006, bringing the total force to 1,324.

Booker is encouraged by the drop in crime but says the city has a long way to go before it can declare victory. He hopes crime rates will continue to fall as the city rolls out the gunshot detection technology. "When I came in, a big consultant told me a 5% to 10% reduction [in crime] is something to celebrate," says Booker. "I want people to see a 50%, 60%, 70% reduction in violent crime."

On a warm day this May [2008], Matt Klapper, a precocious 25-year-old senior adviser, darts into the mayor's office. Standing in front of photos of Martin Luther King and Mahatma Gandhi that hang on the wall, Klapper unfurls a large map of the city on a table. The map is littered with red dots that mark the location of confirmed shootings. The vast majority of the dots, about 80%, are in the city's South Ward. His point: The city is not throwing cameras up everywhere but is placing them in a seven-square mile area where they can help the most. "This area will be saturated with cameras," says Klapper. "It's an area that has bled."

By taking a more targeted approach, Klapper and city officials believe, the surveillance network will reduce crime, while allaying concerns of privacy advocates. "The cost of pulling that trigger is about to go way up," he says.

To further limit the potential for privacy violations, Klapper and other officials have worked with the ACLU to develop a set of rules and standards. Among them: Cameras will not be allowed to peek inside homes, and the footage is only stored for 30 days. "There are a million ways this system could help if it's implemented intelligently," says Peter Lutz, Newark's director of Police Management Information Systems. "That's what's going to make the difference between us and other cities."

A Big Step Up

Booker is doing his best to shake up the city—and especially the police department. In 2006, when he took over from Sharpe James, a flamboyant and controversial figure who had won five straight elections, the police department had suffered from decades of underinvestment and corruption. Cops were writing on chalkboards and poking typewriter keys to file reports. There were nine cameras that no one was watching. "When I walked into our police precincts, I saw scenes that looked like *Barney Miller* [late 1970s TV comedy series set in a police station]," says Booker.

Soon after, he bucked the tradition of his predecessor by hiring an outsider to be his top cop: Garry McCarthy, a veteran of the New York Police Dept. McCarthy brought a higher level of professionalism to the force and rolled out CompStat, a data-centric system created by the NYPD that focuses on quality-of-life infractions and crime hot spots.

Crime began to drop. But in the summer of 2007 the city was convulsed by a triple homicide. Three kids, all of them either in college or on their way that fall, were gunned down in a city schoolyard. It was a turning point for the young administration. "This was just heartbreaking what happened to those children," says Newark Community Foundation board member and former New Jersey Bell CEO Alfred Koeppe. "There was a sense of: What can we do?"

The mayor knew he had to respond forcefully. Days after the killings, Klapper, the young aide, set up a meeting at City Hall with police officials and local leaders to ask them to fund a pilot program for the camera surveillance technology. After hearing the pitch, Arthur Ryan, the former CEO of Prudential Financial, and private equity pioneer Ray Chambers decided to back not just a pilot but the whole program. They agreed to pony up $3.2 million so the city could roll out more than 100 cameras. "It is truly the grandest kind of social investment that I have seen in this city since the 1960s," says Koeppe, who helped broker the investment. Adds Klapper: "It was the best day in my life."

It's that kind of support that gives Don Katz even more comfort in his decision to make a bet on Newark. Now, Katz and other businessmen are hoping that the Newark revival will extend beyond downtown and into the city's more troubled areas. "You are aware that there is a disparity between your sense of safety downtown and some other neighborhoods," says Katz. "If [Mayor] Cory [Booker] has his way, it won't end with downtown."

| "General video surveillance is not effective at fighting crime."

Surveillance Equipment Does Not Reduce Crime

American Civil Liberties Union

In the following viewpoint, the American Civil Liberties Union (ACLU), a nonprofit organization formed to defend the civil rights of all Americans, argues that general video surveillance does not prevent crime. The ACLU is responding to the recent installation of video monitoring equipment in Washington, D.C., which the organization thinks does more harm than good. The ACLU asserts that using surveillance equipment has not been proven effective and actually reduces the number of police officers on the streets of troubled neighborhoods. Furthermore, the ACLU believes that such equipment impairs civil liberties, such as the right to privacy.

As you read, consider the following questions:

1. On average, about how many times per day is the average Londoner captured on the city's 150,000 surveillance cameras?

American Civil Liberties Union, "D.C. Video Cameras vs. Live Community Police in Our Neighborhoods." Reproduced by permission. www.aclu-nca.org.

2. What types of monitoring does general video surveil-lance not include?

3. About how much money was spent on the Washington, D.C. surveillance program in its early stages?

D.C.'s [District of Columbia's] Metropolitan Police Department (MPD) has installed an invasive network of surveillance cameras to spy on D.C. inhabitants and plans to expand it. Though the MPD claims terrorism is the motivating force behind the plan, it was established long before 9-11 [the terrorist attacks of September 11, 2001]. In fact the proposal is not so limited, it doesn't stop terrorism, and its negative consequences are far-reaching, including harming real crime fighting. Cameras would monitor law-abiding residents engaging in their day-to-day routines.

The Metropolitan Police Department's general video surveillance program was initiated well before September 11, 2001. MPD mounted its cameras to track domestic protesters who came to the Nation's Capital to petition the government. It continues to do so today, spying on anti-war demonstrators and pro-life demonstrators alike. The claimed use of general video surveillance to fight terrorism and ordinary crime was an afterthought.

After the *Wall Street Journal* first broke the story on February 13, 2002, that MPD had set up a general video surveillance program, the Mayor and Chief of Police declared that they wanted a British-style system for Washington, D.C. In London, there are 150,000 cameras, so many that on average each person there is captured by the CCTV 300 times in the course of a single day. Do we want a British-style system for our nation's capital? We answer with the words of Justice Louis D. Brandeis: "The right of the people to be let alone [is] the most comprehensive of rights and the right most valued by a civilized [people]." *Olmstead v. United States*, 277 U.S. 438 (1928). But it is now argued that in today's world, we need surveillance cameras. We must sacrifice individual liberty because of the greater need for public safety. This is a false choice.

What Are We Against?

First, let's be clear about what we want the D.C. Council to prohibit: general video surveillance by the District government. This is the government's using surveillance cameras as a dragnet to photograph law-abiding people in public places such as parks, plazas, and sidewalks without regard to any suspicion of wrongdoing. As a fishing expedition, general video surveillance reverses the American presumption of innocence and assumes that everyone is about to commit a crime.

While we may have reservations about being monitored in private buildings such as department stores that use in-store cameras, we can choose not to patronize such establishments. That's different from being spied on by the government in public areas such as parks, where we are entitled to be.

There are focused uses of video technology that do not function as a dragnet over law-abiding persons to which we do not object. General video surveillance does *not* include the use of video technology to:

- Investigate individuals suspected of criminal activity.

- Provide exterior building security.

- Detect those breaking motor vehicle laws (speeding and running red lights), but without photographing occupants of the vehicles.

- Provide real-time traffic control at congestion points, but without recording license plates or individual images.

- Record interactions of police officers and the public using cameras mounted on police cars.

Video Surveillance Does Not Work

We cannot be free if we are not safe. All of us fear being victimized by crime. The District faces a crisis of poor police presence in our neighborhoods. Not only are there not enough officers on patrol, but too often residents can't get through to 911 to get help in an emergency. The *Washington Post* reported (February 12, 2003) that just one 911 operator was on duty on January 15 [2003], the morning a man burned to death while roommates and neighbors tried unsuccessfully to reach 911.

Using MPD funds for surveillance cameras instead of rectifying these problems is a dodge. General video surveillance is not effective at fighting crime.

Any question about the efficacy of surveillance cameras in fighting crime was laid to rest by the August 2002 "Meta Study" of the British Home Office, "Crime Prevention Effects of Closed Circuit Television: A Systematic Review." The Home Office, a proponent of video surveillance technology, reviewed 46 studies including five from the United States that analyzed the cameras' crime fighting value. The bottom line is that in the areas of concern to the District of Columbia—center city and residential areas, video technology has no beneficial effect on reducing crime.

Other American cities, most notably Oakland, California and Detroit, Michigan, considered or tried general video surveillance and decided against it. Oakland Police Chief Joseph Samuels, Jr. stated that his department had hoped to be "among the pioneers in the field of taped video camera surveillance" but ultimately found that "there is no conclusive way to establish that the presence of video surveillance resulted in the prevention or reduction of crime."

We should not credit anecdotal claims that surveillance cameras reduce crime, such as the Baltimore police department makes. A Baltimore official acknowledged at the Council's December 12, 2002 hearing that no study had been

Surveillance Studies Are Inconclusive

Studies in England have been similarly inconclusive. The Home Office's most recent survey evaluated thirteen local surveillance programs, comparing crime rates in areas under surveillance to crime rates in control areas without surveillance. The study found a statistically significant reduction in crime in only one of the thirteen areas that had been under surveillance. (Seven of the thirteen areas had actually seen *increases* in crime rates.)

There is also a dearth of empirical evidence to support the proposition that surveillance cameras deter acts of terrorism. Video cameras recorded some of the movements of the September 11 [2001] hijackers, but—as one observer put it—"those images chiefly served, in the aftermath of the attacks, as a kind of eerie visual diary." Even the omnipresence of CCTV in the London public transport system did not prevent the deaths of fifty-six people in the terrorist attacks of July 2005.

The New York City Civil Liberties Union,
"Who's Watching?: Video Camera Surveillance
in New York City and the Need for Public Oversight,"
Fall 2000. www.nyclu.org.

made that controlled for all the variables that might explain a change in the crime rate. London, which has 150,000 cameras, has experienced a surge in crime. Can we blame the cameras?

Cops Not Cameras

What is needed, as the District Council has recognized, is full staffing of the Police Service Areas—community policing. The National Black Police Association has said: "Camera surveillance funds could be better spent to hire and promote additional officers, and training them to work cooperatively with the public they serve."

The District does not need to study the question whether cameras reduce crime; they don't. Further studies, as proposed in a bill now before the Council, would be wasteful. Studies with adequate controls are expensive. Available funds should better be used to fully staff the PSAs. Indeed the $9 plus million already spent on this project could have paid the first year's salary for about 230 new police officers. The cost of video surveillance is not just the cameras and their installation. Those monitoring the cameras must be paid. Camera advocate and expert, Grant Fredericks, testified at the Judiciary Committee's hearing on December 12th [2002]: "Anything less than 24 hour monitoring and an immediate response could render cameras ineffective." The suggestion that the mere presence of unmonitored cameras deters crime is wrong. . . .

Neighborhood organizations and the ACLU [American Civil Liberties Union] have been pushing the police to use scarce law enforcement funds to put more trained, community-sensitive police in the neighborhoods. Some officials, however, appear to be trying to use video cameras as a new dodge to cover the failure to police the neighborhoods; their new excuse is "wait until we get cameras." But using cameras to fight crime—is a waste of money, diverts neighborhood complaints for another year or two. The ACLU believes that inadequate police presence will only be solved by finally making good on the city's promise for adequate police. Wasting money on ineffective cameras, however much temporary political "cover" they might provide, merely delays getting the police (and other crime-fighting measures like recreation centers, after-school programs, youth employment, etc.) the neighborhoods want.

Not Safe and Not Free

We know that general surveillance cameras do not in fact make us more secure. At best they create a false sense of security, which really makes us less secure. And at the same time, surveillance cameras make us less free.

The surveillance camera industry argues that there is no legal or reasonable expectation of privacy in a public area such as a park or a sidewalk, and therefore cameras in such places do not invade your privacy. That there is a greater expectation of privacy in your home or office than in the street does not mean that there is no expectation of privacy in public places. Consider the following example:

> Put yourself on a park bench reading a personal letter.
>
> You can expect that someone walking behind you might in passing see a word or two. What if that person stopped, leaned forward, and began reading the letter over your shoulder?
>
> That's an invasion of your private space in a public area. It's an invasion of your privacy!
>
> General Video Surveillance cameras are like that.

It's also argued that cameras on a street corner are no different than a police officer on the corner. That's wrong. There are important differences:

> Joe or Suzie, the beat cop, is a physical presence. The officer interacts with you and your family. The community officer's presence is reassuring and effective. Joe or Suzie is there to help you, and the officer turns to you when your cooperation is needed.
>
> When we replace cops with cameras, the quality of life on the street changes. Surveillance cameras are monitored by unknown persons from unknown places. Cameras watch, track, and silently accuse. The police department is no longer the beat cop.

The quality of life on the street changes when you are constantly being monitored by the government. The street is no longer a refuge of anonymity. The mere presence of cameras induces social conformity. This infringes upon liberty in a most fundamental sense.

Surveillance cameras are an invitation to abuse. We know from the British experience that those monitoring cameras engage in racial profiling as they pivot the cameras and zoom in on their targets. Boredom monitoring screens is often relieved by surveillance camera voyeurism: focusing on attractive women and amorous couples. Many call this "video stalking." There have been various reports of police officers using police databases to track down ex-girlfriends or estranged spouses. There's no reason to believe surveillance cameras would be subject to less abuse.

Our altogether natural fear of being victimized by crime makes us predisposed to see surveillance cameras as a solution. But once people know that cameras are not effective at reducing the crime rate, they turn to solutions that do work, namely community policing. The District Council has now insisted that the police department fully staff Police Service Areas to provide neighborhoods the benefits of community policing. Armed with the facts, people understand that cameras diminish security by diverting limited funds from putting officers into our neighborhoods.

The surveillance camera issue is not whether we must sacrifice our freedom to enhance our security. We purchase and install surveillance cameras to the detriment of both our security and our freedom. The Metropolitan Police Department's video surveillance network should be dismantled so that there is no further temptation to use it simply because it's there. We can be safe and free.

Periodical Bibliography

The following articles have been selected to supplement the diverse views presented in this chapter.

America	"Save Lives, and Money, Too," March 16, 2009.
Gary J. Bass	"Humanitarian Impulses," *New York Times Magazine*, August 17, 2008.
Michael Brunton	"Message in a Bottle," *Time Atlantic*, December 18, 2008.
Michelle Conlin	"To Catch a Corporate Thief," *Business Week*, February 16, 2009.
Liz Curran	"Kids or Criminals," *Eureka Street*, September 12, 2008.
Stephanie Dube	"Online Verification: Who Can You Trust in the Virtual World?" *Business Week Online*, January 14, 2009.
Reid Goldsborough	"Avoid Becoming an Internet Victim Through Some Easy Steps," *Community College Week*, January 26, 2009.
Alex Kingsbury	"The War on Gangs," *U.S. News & World Report*, December 15, 2008.
Sara Lipka	"Do Crime Statistics Keep Students Safe?" *Chronicle of Higher Education*, January 30, 2009.
Ken MacQueen et al.	"How to Fight the Gangs," *Maclean's*, March 16, 2009.
Damaso Reyes	"Harlem Takes a Night Out Against Crime," *New York Amsterdam News*, August 7, 2008.
Wilson Quarterly	"Contagious Crime," Winter 2009.

How Can Recidivism Rates Be Reduced?

Chapter Preface

Recidivism, or the relapse into criminal behavior, remains a serious problem. According to the Commission on Safety and Abuse in America's Prisons in June 2006, "within three years, 67 percent of former prisoners will be rearrested and 52 percent will be re-incarcerated." Although in-prison rehabilitation and community support programs might prevent some released criminals from committing future crimes, assisting child sex abusers is another matter altogether. For decades it has been thought that pedophiles could not be rehabilitated, but recent studies have shown that this might not be the case.

It has been believed that people who sexually molest children can never stop. According to former Federal Prosecutor Lis Wiehl on *FoxForum* in July 2008, "A shoplifter can be rehabilitated, a burglar can be rehabilitated, even a murderer can be rehabilitated. But not a pedophile. Once a pedophile, always a pedophile." Her statement echoes years of studies that have shown treatment programs for pedophiles do not work. For example, a 2006 Canadian study tracking released child molesters for twenty years showed that 43 percent reoffended regardless of rehabilitation. Some researchers argue that sex offenders cannot be rehabilitated in part because they can never be entirely removed from the stimulus causing the dysfunctional behavior. Children are everywhere in society. In fact, the belief in the lack of rehabilitation is so pervasive among medical and correctional professionals and the public that there is frequently little attempt to treat these offenders.

Recent studies, however, have shown that there may be hope for child molesters. A study that appeared in the June 2006 *Federal Probation* journal reveals that "treatment programs can contribute to community safety because those who attend and cooperate with program conditions are less likely to re-offend than those who reject interventions." To support these results, two studies, one that followed sex offenders in California and another that tracked them in Minnesota, found that they had low rates of recidivism, even lower than other criminals. According to Peter Aldhous, who reported the findings in the January 24, 2009, *New Scientist*, this new information "will challenge public perceptions about the risks these criminals pose." In other words, rather than assume released sex offenders are automatically going to re-offend, communities should help them find treatment centers and other support systems to prevent future incidents.

Despite these recent findings, no definitive treatment plan for sex offenders has been discovered, and few people are willing to take chances on the safety of their children. Like recidivism in general, which the authors in this chapter explore, finding a solution to integrating released criminals back into society remains a struggle. Nonetheless, scientists and policy makers will continue to seek answers.

> "A comprehensive study of recidivism involves much more than simply reporting rates of re-offending."

Measuring Recidivism Is Complicated

Martha Lyman and Stefan LoBuglio

Martha Lyman is the director of research at the Hampden County Correctional Center, Massachusetts. Stefan LoBuglio is the chief of Pre-Release and Reentry Services Division of Montgomery County Department of Correction and Rehabilitation, Maryland. In the following viewpoint, they argue that measuring the rate at which criminals return to jail, also known as recidivism, is challenging because of multiple factors which impact re-offending. The process of collecting data is further complicated by the lack of a reliable operational definition of recidivism. Keeping accurate recidivism records is important to reducing the crime rate, saving money spent on corrections, and maintaining prison safety.

As you read, consider the following questions:

1. About how much time will the majority of inmates spend in jail?

Martha Lyman and Stefan LoBuglio, "'Whys and Hows' of Measuring Jail Recidivism," Washington, DC: Urban Institute, 2006. © 2006 Urban Institute. Reproduced by permission. www.urban.org.

2. How many more inmates do state and federal prisons house in comparison to the nation's jails?

3. What are the four most common components used to measure recidivism?

At community meetings, budgetary hearings before county commissioners, and even family and social occasions, jail administrators are often asked how frequently inmates in their facilities cycle from release to return, and what, if anything, can be done to slow this revolving door. What seem like simple and logical questions actually prove difficult to answer as few jails track their recidivism rates or evaluate their programs with great precision. While most lack the research staff to undertake such analyses, the more fundamental reason is that they fail to see the relevance of calculating recidivism rates for highly mobile and complex jail populations. Running safe, secure, orderly, and humane institutions consumes the time of most jail administrators, and many would wonder the utility of measuring a statistic for which they exercise so little control over the outcome measure. . . .

Understanding Jail Recidivism

Jail and prison populations differ so significantly that measuring recidivism rates among these populations requires different considerations. The nation's jail population flows like a torrential river with upwards of 12 million individuals moving in and out of institutions annually. The admissions and discharges for jails in one month can be half of those entering and leaving state and federal prisons annually. Most jail inmates will spend only hours or days in the institution before being released to the street or transferred to other institutions, however, an estimated 20% will spend at least one month, 12% at least two months, and 4% will spend more than 6 months. Jails serve a variety of functions in the criminal justice system from holding individuals pre-trial, holding individuals temporarily (juveniles, mentally ill, military, court witnesses, protective custody), holding individuals awaiting transfer to a state or federal agencies (often due to overcrowding), or incarcerating offenders serving post-conviction sentences. In many jurisdictions, offenders sentenced to one year or less serve time in jails although the sentence threshold between serving time locally and serving time in the state system ranges from 0 days sentenced to upwards of 30 months.

In conducting a recidivism analysis, researchers must carefully define that portion of the jail population that is released to the community and which is "at risk" to recidivate. It would be meaningless to calculate the recidivism rates for jail inmates transferred to another correctional authority or who are deported, and their inclusion in a study could understate the true recidivism rate of the population. While in jail serving time for one offense, jail inmates often face additional legal issues related to immigration, pending charges on other cases, or have outstanding detainers and warrants. Recidivism rates can be overstated if the dispositions of these pre-existing involvements with the criminal justice system are treated as new recidivist events post-release.

By contrast, offender flow into the nation's prisons can be likened to a stream into a reservoir with upwards of 700,000 individuals entering and leaving each year into state and federal facilities which combined have twice the average daily count of the country's jails. They serve longer sentences than jail inmates: the average state prison sentence is five years and the average federal sentence is even longer (between 5–10 years). While prison inmates also have complicated legal issues that they continue to face while they are serving time, they come into the institution post-conviction and have more orderly and planned departures. For this population, recidivism studies are more straightforward and common. Some state correctional systems do have research departments that publish recidivism statistics for their systems, and stratify this data by offender type and offense. Typically, they do not produce recidivism rates for individual institutions. In June 2002, the United States Department of Justice's Bureau of Justice Statistics published one of the largest and best known studies that found that among nearly 300,000 prisoners released in 15 states in 1994, 67.5% were rearrested within 3 years, 46.9% were convicted for a new crime and 51.8% were re-incarcerated.

Do high recidivism rates indicate that a correctional system is not working? Few correctional officials would agree, particularly those that manage jails. They take issue with the private sector analogy often used that a business with a two-thirds failure rate would go out of business, and would cite the profound differences between private industry and corrections. Corrections can not select or maintain quality control over the "incoming" raw materials that are sent by the court or by parole, and often has very little time to work and develop these materials into better products before release. With considerable criminological research backing, they would argue that the best predictors of continued criminal involvement are beyond their span of control and include offender's age, criminal history, drug usage, and the families and neighborhoods to which these individuals will return. They might add that such factors as the health of the economy and the enforcement, prosecutorial, and sentencing strategies of police, prosecutors, probation and parole agents, and the courts can negate the beneficial effects of programs and release preparation efforts that they might offer offenders in their facilities. Further, not all jails and prisons incarcerate inmates with similar "risk" profiles, making comparisons of recidivism rates across different inmate populations, different geographical areas, and different corrections systems problematic.

For a jail system, the chief value of recidivism analysis is less as an institutional performance measure than as a diag-

Controlling Crime and Prison Populations: Two Levers

States that want to protect public safety while slowing the growth of their prison populations can pull two basic policy levers: they can divert a greater number of low-risk offenders from prison; they can reduce the length of time that the lowest-risk offenders stay behind bars; and, of course, they can do some combination of the two.

Both options require strong community corrections programs to ensure that offenders in the community remain crime- and drug-free.

Reduce prison admissions	Front-end: Sentencing and diversion	Drug Courts that break the cycle of crime and addiction with frequent drug tests, a continuum of treatment services and increasing penalties for violations.
		Targeted penalty changes that steer selected low-risk offenders to community corrections programs or modify mandatory minimums.
		Comprehensive sentencing guidelines that allow states to decide as a matter of policy which types of offenders should go to prison and which are appropriate for community corrections.
	Back-end: Accountability for parole and probation violations	Intermediate sanctions such as day reporting centers for offenders who break the rules of their release, to ensure that each violation receives a swift, certain and proportionate response.
		Short-term residential facilities for persistent rule violators with substance abuse problems.
		Performance incentives that shorten terms of supervision for offenders who comply with their conditions and fulfill obligations such as victim restitution and child support.

[CONTINUED]

nostic tool to better understand how offenders are flowing throughout a region's criminal justice system and to identify changes. Recidivism research is a valuable tool for making decisions affecting security, classification, movement, programs

---

Controlling Crime and Prison Populations: Two Levers
[CONTINUED]

States that want to protect public safety while slowing the growth of their prison populations can pull two basic policy levers: they can divert a greater number of low-risk offenders from prison; they can reduce the length of time that the lowest-risk offenders stay behind bars; and, of course, they can do some combination of the two.

Both options require strong community corrections programs to ensure that offenders in the community remain crime- and drug-free.

Reduce length of stay	Release: Risk reduction before reentry	Risk reduction credits that allow slightly earlier release for inmates who complete treatment and education programs designed to reduce recidivism.
		Risk-based release instruments that use analysis of actual recidivism patterns to help releasing authorities decide who should remain behind bars and who is ready for release.
		Sufficient program availability in prisons and the community so release isn't delayed because inmates cannot complete requirements.

TAKEN FROM: The Pew Center on the States, "One in 100: Behind Bars in America 2008," www.pewcenteronthestates.org, February 2008.

---

and release planning. It is also useful for tracking population trends, to project staffing needs, allocate resources and form community partnerships. Such analysis helps determine whether correctional resources are being used wisely and whether certain policy and programmatic changes are needed. . . . Also, understanding the recidivists' patterns between different types of offenders can also lead institutions to adopt more targeted program interventions.

Developing baseline recidivism rates for jails by offender characteristics and offense types can also prove helpful in the evaluation of specific education, treatment, and pre-release reentry programs. Increasingly, outside funders and local policy makers will ask jail administrators to demonstrate that their requests for funding for a particular program includes a robust evaluation design that goes well beyond graduation statistics or testimonial letters. They want evaluations to address the rampant problem of self-selection (or creaming) by including a scientific design where the recidivism rates of program participants are compared with a comparable group of offenders that share similar characteristics (control group). While evaluations that randomly assign individuals between treatment and control groups remain the gold standard of evaluation design, they prove very difficult to implement within a correctional setting. However, a quasi-experimental design allows for the use of matched sample of offenders to serve as a control with a treatment group, and institutions that have baseline recidivism statistics categorized in several dimensions can more easily carry out this method. It also addresses the pitfall of many jail program designs that compare the recidivism rates of program participants with national or state recidivism statistics without recognizing the significant differences that exist inherently between different correctional populations.

The Problem of Defining Recidivism

There are a number of significant inconsistencies among recidivism studies that seriously limit their usefulness for comparative analysis between agencies, states or programs. The most problematic of these is the lack of a consistent operational definition of recidivism. The four most common measures for recidivism are re-arrest, re-arraignment, reconviction and re-incarceration. Most studies of state prisons define recidivism as re-incarceration. Many program-based studies use re-arrest, others reconviction. There is also the question of what constitutes re-offending. Most state and federal agencies include technical violations of release conditions (probation or parole), but not all. Most studies do not include recidivistic activity that occurs out of state, largely due to lack of available data. Some state prisons record only re-incarcerations to their facility. In an ideal world, corrections and other criminal justice agencies would utilize a common operational definition of recidivism, but unless and until that occurs, all studies must clearly state the criteria they used to define recidivism. . . .

A comprehensive study of recidivism involves much more than simply reporting rates of re-offending; it requires an examination of the "who, what, when, where, and how" questions related to re-offending. Trying to determine why some individuals return to criminal behavior while others do not is somewhat like assembling a jigsaw puzzle; there is seldom only one causal factor. One shortcoming to publishing an *overall* recidivism rate is that it may mask the effect of personal and environmental influences and certain life circumstances (drug use, school, work, domestic relations, and lack of adequate housing) that significantly influence criminal behavior.

Recidivism data for any single year provides only a static view of a number of dynamic phenomena. Despite this fact, very few agencies conduct *ongoing* recidivism studies. A brief examination of state prison Web sites conducted by the Massachusetts Department of Correction's Research Division in 2004 revealed that fewer than half of the states produce recidivism reports, and even fewer produce them on an annual basis. While one-time studies can be useful in certain circumstances, ongoing studies of recidivism eliminates the risk inherent in relying on one release cohort as "typical" for the inmates from an institution over a long period of time, and can better track the effect of changing external factors on the recidivism rate such as activity by police, courts, prosecutors, parole, economic conditions, and changes in public policy at the local, state and federal level.

| "Drug court programs can reduce recidivism compared to criminal justice alternatives."

Rehabilitation Reduces Recidivism Rates Among Drug Offenders

Government Accountability Office

The Government Accountability Office (GAO) works toward making the federal government accountable to the American public by studying the efficacy of governmental programs. In the following viewpoint, the GAO argues that adult drug courts, which encourage rehabilitation instead of imprisonment for drug offenders, decrease recidivism rates. Although it is unclear from the research if rehabilitation programs prevent addicts from using again, the GAO found that completion of drug treatment programs increased the likelihood that participants would not reoffend.

As you read, consider the following questions:

1. As of September 2004, how many drug court programs were in operation in the United States?

Adult Drug Courts: Evidence Indicates Recidivism Reductions and Mixed Results for Other Outcomes (Background, Results, Concluding Observations). Washington, DC: Government Accountability Office: Report to Congressional Committees, 2005. www.gao.gov.

2. How long is the average minimum participation requirement of most drug court programs?

3. About how much money per participant did the drug courts in this study save the judicial system and potential victims?

Drug court programs were established in the late 1980s as a local response to increasing numbers of drug-related cases and expanding jail and prison populations. These programs are designed to use a court's authority to reduce crime by changing defendants' substance abuse behavior. Under this concept, in exchange for the possibility of dismissed charges or reduced sentences, defendants are diverted to drug court programs in which they agree to participate in judicially monitored substance abuse treatment. Title II of the 21st Century Department of Justice Appropriations Authorization Act reauthorizes the award of federal grants for drug court programs that include court-supervised drug treatment. The award of federal grants to drug court programs was first authorized under Title V of the Violent Crime Control and Law Enforcement Act of 1994.

Study Methods

Drug court programs have become popular nationwide in the criminal justice system. As of September 2004, there were over 1,200 drug court programs operating in addition to about 500 being planned. With such expansion, it is important for policy and operational decision makers to have definitive information about drug court programs' effectiveness in reducing recidivism and substance use relapse. In this respect, the 21st Century Department of Justice Appropriations Authorization Act requires that we study drug court program effectiveness. In response, this report describes the results of published empirical evaluations of adult drug court programs, particularly relating to (1) recidivism outcomes of participants and other comparable offenders, (2) substance use relapse of participants and other comparable offenders, (3) program completion of participants, and (4) costs and benefits of drug court programs.

To address our objectives, we conducted a systematic review of drug court program literature. We identified 117 evaluations of adult drug court programs in the United States that were published between May 1997 and January 2004 and reported recidivism, substance use relapse, or program completion outcomes. Of these 117, we selected 27 evaluations that met additional criteria for methodological soundness. Most of the evaluations we selected used designs in which all drug court program participants were compared with an appropriate group of similar offenders who did not participate in the drug court program. In order to ensure that the groups are similar in virtually all respects aside from the intervention, we selected evaluations in which the comparison group was matched to the program group as closely as possible on a number of characteristics or that used statistical models to adjust, or control for, preexisting differences between the program and comparison groups. Five of the 27 evaluations were experiments in which participants were randomly assigned to groups. Random assignment works to ensure that the groups are comparable.

The 27 evaluations we selected for our review reported information on 39 unique adult drug court programs. We systematically collected information from these evaluations about the methodological characteristics of the evaluations, the participants and components of the drug court programs, the outcomes, and, where available, the costs of the drug court programs. To assess the methodological strength of the evaluations, we used generally accepted social science principles. Additionally, we used standard cost-benefit criteria to screen and assess the eight evaluations that reported cost and benefit information. Four of these contained sufficient data on costs and benefits to allow us to assess net benefits. We selected the evaluations in our review according to the strength of their methodologies; therefore, our results cannot be generalized to all drug court programs or their evaluations. Finally, we interviewed drug court researchers and officials at the Department of Justice, the National Institute on Drug Abuse, and the Office of National Drug Control Policy (ONDCP). We conducted our work from October 2003 through February 2005 in accordance with generally accepted government auditing standards. . . .

The Limitations of Previous Studies

Of the 1,700 drug court programs operating or planned as of September 2004, about 1,040—nearly 770 operating and about 270 being planned—were adult drug court programs, according to data collected by the Office of Justice Programs' Drug Court Clearinghouse and Technical Assistance Project. The primary purpose of these programs is to use a court's authority to reduce crime by changing defendants' substance abuse behavior. In exchange for the possibility of dismissed charges or reduced sentences, eligible defendants who agree to participate are diverted to drug court programs in various ways and at various stages in the judicial process. These programs are typically offered to defendants as an alternative to probation or short-term incarceration.

Drug court programs share several general characteristics but vary in their specific policies and procedures because of, among other things, differences in local jurisdictions and criminal justice system practices. In general, judges preside over drug court proceedings, which are called status hearings; monitor defendants' progress with mandatory drug testing; and prescribe sanctions and rewards as appropriate in collaboration with prosecutors, defense attorneys, treatment providers, and others. Drug court programs also vary in terms of the substance abuse treatment required. However, most programs

Case Study: The Delaware Department of Correction

The Delaware Department of Correction conducts both institutional and transitional drug treatment programs. Institutional programs, called the Key program for men and WCI Village (Women's Correctional Institute) for women, provide treatment in a therapeutic community over at least a 12-month period. The WCI Village contracts with the private sector to provide treatment services in a building on the grounds of the women's correctional facility. The coed transitional support services program, called the Crest program, provides work-release activities or a halfway house setting with drug treatment. A study of the programs indicates that abusers who participate in a combination of the programs have the most success at remaining drug and arrest free, whereas abusers who receive no treatment have the highest failure rates.

Findings of Delaware Department of Correction programs at 6- and 18-month postrelease

	6-month followup		18-month followup	
	Drug free	Arrest free	Drug free	Arrest free
Comparison group	35%	62%	19%	30%
Key group	70	82	30	48
Crest group	85	85	45	65
Key Crest group	95	97	76	71

Source: National Institute of Justice, A Corrections-based Continuum of Effective Drug Abuse Treatment, Washington, DC: U.S. Department of Justice, June 1996.

TAKEN FROM: Office of National Drug Control Policy, "Drug Treatment in the Criminal Justice System," www.whitehousedrugpolicy.gov, March 2001.

offer a range of treatment options and generally require a minimum of about 1 year of participation before a defendant completes the program.

In order to determine defendants' eligibility for participation, drug court programs typically screen defendants based on their legal status and substance use. The screening process and eligibility criteria can vary across drug court programs. According to the literature, eligible drug court program participants ranged from nonviolent offenders charged with drug-related offenses who have substance addictions to relatively medium-risk defendants with fairly extensive criminal histories and failed prior substance abuse treatment experiences. Participants were also described as predominantly male with poor employment and educational achievements. . . .

Research on drug court programs has generally focused on program descriptions and process measures, such as program completion rates, and presented limited empirical evidence about the effectiveness of drug court programs in reducing recidivism and substance use. In 1997, we reported on 12 evaluations that met minimum research standards and concluded that the evaluations showed some positive results but did not firmly establish whether drug court programs were successful in reducing offender recidivism and substance use relapse. More recently, two syntheses of multiple drug court program evaluations have drawn positive conclusions about the impact of drug court programs. One synthesis concluded that criminal activity and substance use are reduced relative to other comparable offenders while participants are engaged in the drug court program, and that program completion rates ranged from 36 to 60 percent. Further, the other synthesis reported that drug offenders participating in a drug court program are less likely to re-offend than similar offenders sentenced to traditional correctional options, such as probation.

Some of the evaluations included in these two syntheses had methodological limitations such as the lack of strong comparison groups and the lack of appropriate statistical controls. Some did not use designs that compared all drug court program participants—including graduates, those still active, and dropouts—with similar nonparticipants. For example, they compared the outcomes of participants who completed the program with the outcomes of those who did not (that is, dropouts). These evaluations, upon finding that program graduates had better outcomes than dropouts, have concluded that drug court programs are effective. This is a likely overestimation of the positive effects of the intervention because the evaluation is comparing successes to failures, rather than all participants to nonparticipants. Additionally, other evaluations did not use appropriate statistical methods to adjust for preexisting differences between the program and comparison groups. Without these adjustments, variations in measured outcomes for each group may be a function of the preexisting differences between the groups, rather than the drug court program.

Adult Drug Court Programs Work

In most of the evaluations we reviewed, adult drug court programs led to recidivism reductions during periods of time that generally corresponded to the length of the drug court program—that is, within-program. Our analysis of evaluations reporting recidivism data for 23 programs showed that lower percentages of drug court program participants than comparison group members were rearrested or reconvicted. Program participants also had fewer incidents of rearrests or reconvictions and a longer time until rearrest or reconviction than comparison group members. These recidivism reductions were observed for any felony offense and for drug offenses, whether they were felonies or misdemeanors. However, we were unable to find conclusive evidence that specific drug court program components, such as the behavior of the judge, the amount of treatment received, the level of supervision provided, and the sanctions for not complying with program requirements, affect participants' within-program recidivism. Post-program recidivism reductions were measured for up to 1 year after participants completed the drug court program in several evaluations, and in these the evidence suggests that the recidivism differences observed during the program endured. . . .

Evidence about the effectiveness of drug court programs in reducing participants' substance use relapse is limited and mixed. The evidence included in our review on substance use relapse outcomes is limited to data available from eight drug court programs. The data include drug test results and self-reported drug use; both measures were reported for some programs. Drug test results generally showed significant reductions in use during participation in the program, while self-reported results generally showed no significant reductions in use. . . .

Completion rates, which refer to the number of individuals who successfully completed a drug court program as a percentage of the total number admitted, in the programs we reviewed that assessed completion ranged from 27 to 66 percent. As might be expected, program completion was associated with participants' compliance with program requirements. Specifically, evaluations of 16 adult drug court programs that assessed completion found that participants' compliance with procedures was consistently associated with completion. These program procedures include attending treatment sessions, engaging in treatment early in the program, and appearing at status hearings. No other program factor, such as the severity of the sanction that would be invoked if participants failed to complete the program and the manner in which judges conducted status hearings, predicted participants' program completion. Several characteristics of the drug court program participants themselves were also associated with an increased likelihood of program completion. These characteristics include lower levels of prior involvement in the criminal justice system and age, as older participants were more likely to complete drug court programs than younger ones. . . .

A limited number of evaluations in our review discussed the costs and benefits of adult drug court programs. Four evaluations of seven drug court programs provided sufficient cost and benefit data to estimate their net benefits (that is, the benefits minus costs). The cost per drug court program participant was greater than the cost per comparison group member in six of these drug court programs. However, all seven programs yielded positive net benefits, primarily from reductions in recidivism affecting both judicial system costs and avoided costs to potential victims. Net benefits ranged from about $1,000 per participant to about $15,000 in the seven programs. These benefits may underestimate drug court programs' true benefits because the evaluations did not include indirect benefits (such as reduced medical costs of treated participants). Financial cost savings for the criminal justice system (taking into account recidivism reductions) were found in two of the seven programs. . . .

Completion of Programs Is Essential

Overall, positive findings from relatively rigorous evaluations in relation to recidivism, coupled with positive net benefit results, albeit from fewer studies, indicate that drug court programs can be an effective means to deal with some offenders. These programs appear to provide an opportunity for some individuals to take advantage of a structured program to help them reduce their criminal involvement and their substance abuse problems, as well as potentially provide a benefit to society in general.

Although not representative of all drug court programs, our review of 27 relatively rigorous evaluations provides evidence that drug court programs can reduce recidivism compared to criminal justice alternatives, such as probation. These results are consistent with those of past reviews of drug court evaluations. Positive results concerning recidivism are closely associated with program completion. Specifically, while drug court participation is generally associated with lower recidivism, the recidivism of program completers is lower than for participants in comparison or control groups. Thus, practices that encourage program completion may enhance the success of drug court programs in relation to recidivism.

While our review sheds little light on the specific aspects of these programs that are linked to positive recidivism outcomes, both participant compliance with drug court procedures and some participant characteristics seem to be related to success. To the extent that research can help to discern best practices for drug courts, the models for effective programs can be enhanced. Specifically, to the extent that drug court program managers can learn more about methods to retain participants for the duration of the program, they may be able to further enhance the positive impacts of drug court programs.

| "*Everyone involved in corrections. . . . must be held responsible for reducing recidivism rates.*"

Corrections Officials Should Be Held Responsible for Recidivism

Jason Newman

Jason Newman is the state and local policy director at the Democratic Leadership Council, which seeks to advance progressive ideals through scholarship and governmental reform. In the following viewpoint, he argues that corrections officials should be held responsible for lowering recidivism rates. Newman recommends that this project can be accomplished by integrating a computerized system to track inmates in and out of prison, increasing the amount of money available to communities with high rates of ex-offenders, and increasing parole and probation officers' power.

As you read, consider the following questions:

1. Approximately how many inmates are released from prison each year?

Jason Newman, "Stop Revolving-Door Justice: How Corrections Systems Can Reduce Recidivism," *Progressive Policy Institute*, July 2008, pp. 1–11. Reproduced by permission. www.ppionline.org.

2. By what percentage did New York murder rates fall between 1993 and 1998?

3. What percentage of state prisoners do not have high school diplomas?

Prisons in the United States are full to overflowing. More than one in every 100 adult Americans are now in prison or jail—the highest rate in our nation's history. Whether the United States locks up "too many" people is an interesting and contentious question. What is beyond dispute, however, is this: The more offenders we put behind bars, the more who will eventually be sent home. In fact, 95 percent of prisoners will one day get out, and released prisoners have unleashed a crime wave in many U.S. communities.

Approximately 650,000 inmates are released from prison each year. According to the Bureau of Justice Statistics (BJS), two-thirds of them will be rearrested, and over half will return to prison within three years. In fact, parolees accounted for more than 35 percent of the people entering prison in 2000, almost double the proportion from two decades ago.

In addition to the number of individuals on parole— which at the end of 2006 numbered just short of 800,000— there were more than 4.2 million on probation, leaving more than 5 million ex-offenders under some sort of community supervision (1 million more than in 1995). Add to that the more than 2 million people in jail or prison in 2006, and the total number of offenders in the corrections system totaled 7.2 million, the highest ever. In contrast, only 1.8 million people were in the corrections system in 1980.

Such statistics put America's corrections system in the spotlight. While criminals are locked up, the system does too little to prepare them to be reintegrated into their communities as productive, law-abiding citizens. And it fails to effectively supervise people on probation and parole, even though their propensity to commit more crimes is well known.

The escalating crime rate among discharged prisoners also highlights a basic defect in conservatives' reflexively punitive approach to law enforcement. Their disdain for prisoner rehabilitation guarantees that most offenders will simply be dumped back into the communities they came from, without the skills, tools and incentives they need to change their lives. In their zeal to punish the wicked, many conservatives have lost sight of public safety.

Progressives should not shy from tough sentences for cold-blooded predators and drug profiteers, even if that means high incarceration rates. At the same time, however, they should insist that the U.S. corrections system be tasked with *preventing* crime as well as punishing it after the fact. In practice, this means that everyone involved in corrections—wardens, sheriffs, parole officers, and probation supervisors—must be held responsible for reducing recidivism rates.

Three-Step Solution

Specifically, PPI [Progressive Policy Institute] proposes three steps to fix our broken corrections system:

1. Develop and implement a CompStat-like system for federal and state corrections. CompStat (short for computer statistics) is the crime-data tracking system New York City used to achieve a spectacular reduction in violent crime in the 1990s. A CompStat for corrections would measure and publicize the recidivism rates of inmates discharged from specific institutions, as well as those on probation or parole. This would give corrections officials a powerful new tool for comparing the performance of the people in charge of these institutions, and holding them accountable for measurable improvements.

2. Create a new Office of Community Supervision (OCS) within the U.S. Department of Justice. An OCS would make grants to local parole and probation departments, with the goal of doubling the number of parole and probation officers in communities where ex-offenders are concentrated. An OCS might even place juvenile probation officials directly in schools that have high concentrations of young people at risk of incarceration.

3. In return for federal help, communities should give their parole and probation officers the power to impose more effective sanctions on violators. The current regimen of spotty, unpredictable punishments for those who break the rules of their probation or parole clearly is not working. Probation officers also need the authority and resources to monitor the position of newly-released offenders, and to administer drug tests more frequently. The bottom line is that individuals on probation and parole should be held responsible for their own successful return to free society, and we need to establish strong guidelines to help drive home that fundamental point.

These proposals build on successful crime-fighting innovations that helped reduce U.S. crime rates in the 1990s. For example, President Bill Clinton's Community Oriented Policing Services (COPS) initiative put well over 100,000 new police officers on the beat in localities that agreed to deploy them in community policing. At around the same time, New York City Police Commissioner Bill Bratton instituted CompStat to track crime statistics precinct by precinct. This highly specific data enabled the department to see exactly when and where crime was happening—and to hold police commanders accountable for stopping it. Together with community policing and other reforms, CompStat worked: Murders in New York fell 68 percent between 1993 and 1998, while the overall number of felonies was cut in half.

Unfortunately, in his very first budget, President [George W.] Bush sought to gut funding for the COPS hiring program. While congressional Democrats parried such efforts for a while, the COPS budget steadily declined and by 2006 had been "zeroed out." Partisan animus probably played a role, but Republicans also seem to have been motivated by their party's habitual hostility to federal activism. Criminal justice, they pointed out, is overwhelmingly a state and local responsibility.

This assertion is true, but while crime may be a local responsibility, it is also a national problem that demands a forceful response from the nation's leaders. For one thing, the federal government operates a big prison system of its own, with approximately 200,000 inmates. In addition, the rise of nationwide gang networks and the interstate preparations of the September 11 [2001] terrorists should erase any doubt about the legitimacy of a robust federal role in our nation's law-enforcement efforts. An analogy may be drawn to public education, also largely a state and local matter, but one in which Washington (under both Democratic and Republican administrations) has assumed an important strategic role in aiding poor districts, raising performance standards, and encouraging reform. In this spirit, Clinton carved out a limited but constructive federal role in using small amounts of money to leverage major innovations in policing.

The Progressive Policy Institute believes it is time to extend the same principle to America's corrections system, including both the adult and juvenile systems. Taking up where Clinton left off, our next president should encourage the states to use information technology to break down bureaucratic barriers between various parts of the corrections system, measure that system's performance, and hold officials accountable for results.

An Ex-Con Crime Wave

Over the last several decades, a confluence of factors—public alarm over rising crime rates, a surging youth population, the crack epidemic, and mandatory-sentence laws—have combined to produce today's record-breaking incarceration rates. Since 95 percent of inmates are eventually set free, this "get tough" policy has also triggered a record-breaking flow of released prisoners back into our communities. In fact, the num-

Offender Workforce Development Programs Work

When the US Probation Office for the Eastern District of Missouri initiated an offender workforce development program in 2000, the unemployment rate of the persons under its supervision decreased by 52 percent over the next four years. By the end of fiscal year 2003, the rate of convicted persons incarcerated for violating a condition of supervision in this district was 28 percent lower than the federal average, despite a 54 percent increase in the number of persons they supervised.

Paying attention to employment and supporting an offender's return to the workforce does make a difference.

John Rakis, "How to Jam Prison's Revolving Door,"
Christian Science Monitor, *April 6, 2005.*

ber of people released from state prisons each year has grown steadily from approximately 200,000 in 1983, to 400,000 in 1994, to 650,000 in 2005.

Once per decade, the BJS tracks released prisoners from prison in a given year to study their recidivism rates. According to the most recent BJS study of prisoners released in 1994, more than two-thirds (67.5 percent) were rearrested within three years for a new offense (almost exclusively a felony or a serious misdemeanor); 46.9 percent were reconvicted; and 25.4 percent were resentenced. Overall, 51.8 percent were back in prison for some reason within three years.

These numbers were up from a 1983 BJS study, which found that 62.5 percent had been rearrested and 41.4 percent were back in prison within three years. . . . As the number of people released from prison continues to rise, they will account for a growing share of new crimes.

Our overmatched parole and probation systems are failing to supervise these individuals effectively or integrate them into lawful and productive roles in their communities. Consider these facts about current and former prisoners:

- Approximately 68 percent of state prisoners lack a high-school diploma and only about one out of three receive vocational training at any point during incarceration;

- About half are functionally illiterate;

- Three in four have a substance-abuse problem, but only 10 percent receive formal treatment prior to release; and

- An estimated 60 percent of the total volume of heroin and cocaine consumed in this country is sold to those on probation or parole.

Not only are our communities and our citizens drastically less safe because of our failure to properly supervise ex-prisoners, but the state eventually foots a substantially higher bill when they end up back in prison. While costs vary by state, Patrick Kelly and Don Stemen noted in a Vera Institute of Justice report that "it costs upwards of $22,000 a year to confine an individual in jail or prison, as compared with as little as $200 per year to supervise an individual on probation or parole." While the costs in some states are higher than these estimates, the difference between the cost of confining someone to prison versus supervising them in the community is significant. Therefore, lowering the crime rate among former prisoners would not only protect Americans from crime, it would also reap sizeable savings in criminal-justice costs.

Corrections and Crime-Fighting

U.S. political leaders are beginning to zero in on the nation's broken corrections system. In his new book, *A Time to Fight*, Sen. Jim Webb (D-Va.) argues that it is time to "reshape our own [criminal-justice] system in a way that better serves individual justice, community safety, and the long-term productivity of those who have found themselves on the wrong side of the law."

Unfortunately, over the last few decades rehabilitation programs in prisons across the country have been drastically cut. A recent report from California Gov. Arnold Schwarzenegger's Rehabilitation Strike Team found that of the $43,300 spent on each prisoner yearly, just 5 percent is spent on rehabilitation programs. Half of the individuals leaving prisons in California did not participate in *any* rehabilitation or work program or have any type of work assignment during their entire prison term. Similarly, drastic cuts in rehabilitation programs have occurred across the country.

In April 2008, President Bush signed the Second Chance Act of 2007 to help ex-offenders successfully reenter communities and avoid recidivism. The new law will, among other things, expand reentry projects to provide expanded services to offenders, including an initiative to ensure that each inmate released from prison has information on health, employment, personal finance, release requirements, and community resources. In addition, the Crime Control and Prevention Act of 2007, introduced by [former] Sen. Joe Biden (D-Del.), includes new programs for the reduction of recidivism and the successful reintroduction of ex-offenders into the community.

[Former] Sens. Hillary Clinton (D-N.Y.) and Barack Obama (D-Ill.) were both cosponsors of the Senate version of the Second Chance Act of 2007. On the campaign trail, Sen. Obama has called for ensuring that ex-offenders have access to job training, counseling, and employment opportunities. He has also called for the creation of a prison-to-work incentive program. Sen. Clinton seeks a review of sentencing policies, and has called for second-chance programs for non-violent offenders. Recently, [Sen.] Clinton detailed her plan, "Solutions for Safe and Secure Communities Now," which would update the COPS program, set up a $1 billion anti-recidivism program, renew the ban on assault weapons, double the number of at-risk children in after-school programs, and expand early-intervention mentoring programs.

All of these efforts will help, but they do not go far enough. To break the cycle of revolving-door justice, we need to transform America's corrections system using the same tools that modernized policing in the 1990s. . . .

Just as the prison population has grown dramatically over the last couple of decades, so have the ranks of Americans on probation and parole. The costs to our society have risen as well, not only in terms of dollars but also in terms of the rising incidence of crime among individuals who cycle into and out of our criminal-justice system.

It is time that we take a serious look at how to make those responsible for supervising criminal populations more effective at our ultimate goal—reducing crime and making our communities safer. Utilizing some of the same effective practices that helped transform policing in the 1990s we should use information technology to break down bureaucratic barriers between various parts of the corrections system, measure the performance of officials in those systems, and hold these officials accountable for results. In addition, we need to double the number of parole and probation officers, get them out on the streets, and give them the resources to do their jobs effectively. Finally, and most importantly, we must implement a strict accountability system that holds offenders responsible for turning their lives around.

> *"My bet is that all civilized western so-*
> *cieties will eventually reject retributive*
> *justice."*

Restorative Justice Is More Effective than Retribution in Preventing Recidivism

Jonathan Aitken

In the following viewpoint, Jonathan Aitken, a former member of the British Parliament who served eighteen months in prison for perjury, argues that restorative justice is a better solution to preventing criminals from re-offending than retribution. After spending time touring Texas prisons, he concludes that prisoners who were given the opportunity for rehabilitation had far lesser rates of recidivism than those who were sent to prison solely for punishment. He adds that programs like the one found at Carol Vance prison are being opened in London, which makes him optimistic for the future of prison reform.

As you read, consider the following questions:

1. During a seven-year span, how many prisoners released from Carol Vance prison re-offended?

Jonathan Aitken, "Stop Punishing Criminals, It Doesn't Work," *Sunday Times* (London), April 25, 2004. Reproduced by permission of News International Syndication.

2. What does *metanoia* mean?

3. Describe a typical day for prisoners enrolled in IFI programs.

Stoker was incorrigible, firmly set in his wicked ways. Pete was impressionable and potentially changeable. Both were prisoners in their late twenties. I met them in HMP Stanford Hill [prison in London] while serving part of my seven-month sentence for perjury.

Their subsequent histories illuminate the growing debate on the best way to run our system of justice: should we be seeking retribution, or would we see better results—fewer criminals—if we concentrated on restorative justice, which asks prisoners to face up to the damage they have done and make amends.

Stoker was "doing a three" for burglary. It was his fifth time in prison. He told me it was "easy gravy" because he would be out after 18 months and would return to the only way of life he knew would finance his £500-a-week drug habit—more burglaries. He thought he might have committed 500 of these crimes. Words like rehabilitation or restoration to victims meant nothing to him. Stoker is now back in jail in a pattern of recidivism that will probably stay with him for the rest of his life.

Pete was a kiter. That's a fraudster who bounces so many cheques (and stolen credit cards) that they fly around like kites. While serving his four-year term in jail, he had been on several courses including Prison Alpha and a victim awareness programme based on restorative justice principles.

Pressed by his Asian family, Pete did some remorseful rethinking about the consequences of his crimes—not least on his victims. He'd been uncomfortably confronted by them in the form of role-playing actors during the victim awareness course. Somewhere along the line, Pete made a decision to try to go straight. So far, 3 years after leaving prison, he has succeeded.

American Alternatives

In America the retributive versus restorative justice argument is running all the way to the White House. I recently visited two very different prisons in Texas which symbolise the rival concepts of justice. The Carol Vance prison unit at Sugarland near Houston, with 330 inmates, is a showcase for restorative justice. Opened in April 1997 by the then governor of Texas, George W. Bush, the Sugarland jail has been pioneering an innovative regime of education and training known as the innerchange freedom initiative (IFI). According to a recent study, inmates released over the past seven years have reoffended at the rate of 8%.

"I have visited many prisons but this one is completely different," said congressman Tom DeLay, the majority leader of the US House of Representatives [in 2004], as we walked round the IFI buildings the other day. "It is clean, there are no unpleasant smells and you get lots of smiles from inmates."

No visitor could possibly pay the same compliments to Mountain View Penitentiary near Gatesville, Texas. This old-fashioned institution reflects the primitive spirit of retributive justice. It is a high-security women's prison holding 600 inmates with a repeat offending rate of between 65% and 70%—a figure that closely approximates recidivism levels among British prisoners.

After two days visiting Mountain View I drove away from its gaunt watchtowers and 20ft barbed-wire fences with feelings of profound sadness and futility.

There was one particularly poignant moment when one of the volunteers from the charity Prison Fellowship said to the audience: "Will any of you who are moms please stand up."

More than 250 of the 300 white-uniformed prisoners got to their feet. Most were so young and looked so woebegone that my wife Elizabeth and I, along with several other visitors, choked up.

The women of Mountain View are mainly non-violent offenders serving sentences (many of them mandatory terms) of between three and 30 years for crimes from shoplifting and embezzlement to bank fraud and drug dealing.

Like their British equivalents who end up in jails such as Holloway, these inmates tend to have bad records. But is there no better way than judicial toughness for encouraging such prisoners to break out of their depressing life cycles of crime, imprisonment, reoffending and reimprisonment?

Changing Views of Imprisonment

Until recently the general consensus among American jurists and politicians was that tougher sentencing was the best way of dealing with criminals. The leading intellectual advocate for this philosophy of retributive justice, Professor James Q. Wilson, author of *The Moral Sense*, has questioned the very notion of rehabilitation: "Empty a prison in California," he says, "and ask yourself: 'what are these people going to do?' They are not going to give up crime."

But with a US prison population of more than 2m [million] and rising, many opinion formers are exploring new ideas for cutting recidivism.

Restorative justice is a systematic response to wrongdoing that emphasises healing the wounds of victims, offenders and communities. It requires restoration to victims in cash or in kind and sincere repentance by offenders. Repentance in this context goes back to the Greek word *metanoia*, which translates far more richly than in English as "a change of heart and mind".

Retributive justice rarely focuses on healing, victims, communities, restoration, or changes of heart and mind. During

National Recidivism Rates

Percent of released prisoners rearrested within 3 years, by offense, 1983 and 1994

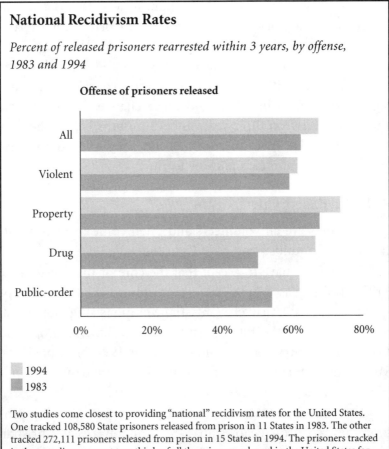

Offense of prisoners released

1994
1983

Two studies come closest to providing "national" recidivism rates for the United States. One tracked 108,580 State prisoners released from prison in 11 States in 1983. The other tracked 272,111 prisoners released from prison in 15 States in 1994. The prisoners tracked in these studies represent two-thirds of all the prisoners released in the United States for that year.

TAKEN FROM: U.S. Department of Justice, Office of Justice Programs, Bureau of Justice Statistics, *Reentry Trends in the U.S.*, October 25, 2002, www.ojp.usdoj.gov.

my prison sentence I met many young villains who had no sense of moral responsibility because they thought their crimes were against the government or property. It did not occur to them that their burglaries or muggings might have traumatised human beings. Restorative justice puts awareness of damage to victims and communities at the top of the agenda, often in confrontational discussion settings.

"IFI programmes are the toughest way to do time in Texas," says Warden Fred Becker, the State Corrections Department official with overall responsibility for the Sugarland complex. A prisoner's day starts at 5:30am and is filled for the next 16 hours with training classes and group seminars designed to develop life skills and inner change. Prisoners start the course between three years and 18 months before their release. They also have to commit to a one-year post-release programme of aftercare and mentoring.

A Faith-Based Curriculum

IFI prisoners are all volunteers and often come from very different backgrounds.

But they all have to accept that the core of their restorative justice training is a faith-based curriculum. IFI training programmes are pervasively Christian, emphasising the moral values taught in the Bible. Hymn singing, Bible readings and prayers are central to daily life, which in 1997 prompted The *Wall Street Journal* to label the newly opened institution a "Bible boot camp".

The organisation that runs and pays for the training programmes is Prison Fellowship, a $50 million-a-year Christian ministry in 105 countries. The founder, Charles W. Colson, was a former White House aide to President Richard Nixon who served a seven-month prison sentence in 1974 for Watergate-related offences. Colson is unfazed by those who oppose the IFI programmes because of their Christian slant. "That 8% reoffending figure tells its own story," he says.

Secular restorative justice courses are now being tried from Tasmania to the Thames Valley. I recently observed the Sycamore Tree courses at HMP High Point in Suffolk where one of the organisers told me, "we talk secular but we think spiritual".

In America today the IFI prisons and their restorative justice courses have a surprising champion in President George

W. Bush. He is evidently a convert from the retributive justice school of thinking that he appeared to uphold with hardline zealotry in his years as governor of Texas. Yet appearances must have been deceptive: it was the same Bush whom Colson persuaded to launch the first IFI prison in 1997.

"The president became worried about the expenditure of $80,000 a year on prisoners, most of whom were back behind bars within three years," said Jim Towey, director of the White House office for faith-based and community initiatives. "He came to see that nothing would change unless the spiritual poverty of such men was addressed." Bush has since asked Congress to allocate $300 million to help 50,000 newly released prisoners to find jobs and housing.

Yet despite these stirrings of reform, in both Britain and America the status quo remains primarily a system of retributive justice.

This was painfully brought home to me when I visited death row at Mountain View on Easter Sunday and met a lady I shall call Agnes. She had committed murder at the age of 21. After 18 years all her avenues for clemency are finally exhausted. In a few weeks she will be driven across the state to Huntsville, the only prison in Texas with an execution chamber, to die by lethal injection—the ultimate act of retributive justice.

My bet is that all civilised western societies will eventually reject retributive justice. At least a start is being made along this road.

| "The program is designed to allow offenders to take responsibility for their lives."

Transition Programs Reduce Recidivism Rates

Danny L. Jordan

In the following viewpoint, Danny L. Jordan discusses the transition program that he implemented as the county administrator in Jackson County in Medford, Oregon. The point of the program is to help offenders re-integrate back into the community successfully to avoid re-offending. It is a short-term, residential program that has three tracts: work restitution, work release, and work release/transition. Participants move through each tract under the supervision of a case worker. While still in its early stages, the program holds promise, according to Jordan. He has seen employment rates rise and drug use decrease among participants.

As you read, consider the following questions:

1. Name the six settings that criminals might encounter after being convicted in Jackson County Oregon.

2. How many hours of public service are all program participants required to complete?

3. What percentage of program participants have found or maintained full-time employment since its inception?

In summary, the [transition] program is designed to be a short-term residential program. It is structured to provide offenders with access to a combination of interventions and services based upon evidence-based principles. The design is intended to maximize the chance of success in the community and minimize the likelihood of recidivism. . . .

The program is designed to allow offenders to take responsibility for their lives through restitution to the community, employment, financial management, drug and alcohol treatment, cognitive restructuring, positive peer association development, and prosocial behavior. Offenders seek employment, participate on work crews, address treatment needs, and transition to the community, while being supported in the change process by an assigned case manager.

A "Middle Ground"

The program serves as the "middle ground" between incarceration and supervision in the community. It is not meant to serve only as a sanction, but rather an option based on principles of combining interventions that likely lead to an increased reduction in recidivism. The program serves as an alternative to incarceration and/or as housing for offenders in need of subsidized placement.

According to Bill Davidson, Ph.D. (2006), the program is based on the idea that there are key areas that contribute to continued criminal careers. Most important among these are:

- Employment.

- Stable housing.

- Illegal substance and alcohol abuse.

- Faulty thinking.

- Restitution to the community.

In order to address these factors, the program is constructed with a number of components. Each component is designed to address one or more of the key areas that contribute to continued criminal careers. Individuals participate in each component based on their risk level and needs as assessed using a validated risk and needs assessment tool. The key components align with the eight principles of evidence-based practices and are:

- Risk and needs assessment with case plan.

- Defined goals and expectations.

- Weekly case review and case staffing.

- Progression in a level system.

- Employment seeking and job placement.

- Education and job training.

- Skills training.

- Financial management.

- Drug and alcohol treatment.

- Cognitive restructuring.

- Medical care.

- Positive peer association development.

- Individual and group treatment.

- Transition activities.

Offenders convicted of crimes and sentenced to 12 months or less to the custody of the local Oregon supervisory authority, and/or those requiring subsidized living arrangements are placed in the most appropriate setting. Offenders serve portions of their sentences within many potential settings as alternatives to being incarcerated. From the most restrictive to the least restrictive, the continuum of settings available generally includes:

- County jail.

- Transition program.

- Electronic surveillance.

- Day reporting (daily check-in/itinerary monitoring).

- Community service.

- Community-based supervision.

Offenders enter the system at the most appropriate point as determined by the local supervisory authority. Offenders "slide" up or down on the continuum as their behavior and progress warrant.

Developing a Case Plan

The program is designed to provide offenders with services to voluntarily meet compliance with court orders and parole and probation supervision, and/or to serve as a subsidy housing placement. The program is designed to provide a minimum level of security in which offenders in the program are not incarcerated and have the physical ability to leave the facility at any time, but where movements in and out of the facility are closely monitored. Offenders may be placed in the program voluntarily—

- After probation supervision revocation,

- As a sanction for violation of conditions of probation, parole or post-prison supervision,

- As an initial condition of supervision,

- For a period of transition from jail or prison,

- By court order, and

- As a subsidy (housing) placement.

Each offender is subject to a complete assessment of his or her needs upon arrival at the program. A case plan determines the specific measurable goals to address individual needs during the stay in the program. The case plan is developed during an interview (staffing) between the offender, a case manager known as a Community Justice Officer (CJO), and the offender's supervising parole and probation officer, if applicable. The offender meets at least weekly with his or her assigned CJO during the stay in the program to assess progress and make appropriate modifications to the plan. Prior to release, the case is reviewed with the offender to develop a plan for discharge.

Treatment programs and skills classes are also offered to assist offenders to take responsibility for their lives through restitution to the community, employment, financial management, treatment, conformance to the laws, compliance with conditions of the program, and ultimately, conditions of formal supervision. Offenders earn privileges as they display consistent, responsible behavior and progress on agreed upon goals. They may earn early discharge to less restrictive alternatives to incarceration in the community if they make sufficient progress. Offenders may receive consequences for misconduct and may be removed from the program if their behavior warrants.

Operations and programs are designed to accustom offenders to the patterns and expectations of a "normal, law-abiding lifestyle." All offenders are expected to be involved in a minimum of 40 hours per week of work restitution in the community, and/or any other approved combination of employment, treatment, and activities. In addition, offenders are responsible, under program staff supervision, for the daily maintenance and cleanliness of the facility. In order to make restitution to the community as a whole for their criminal conduct, all offenders are required as directed to complete at least four hours per week of public service, or more if they are enrolled in the work-crew restitution portion of the program. This service is not to be credited toward any hours ordered as a requirement of the releasing authority.

Program staff is responsible for maintaining the daily operation of the program including the safety and security of offenders. Upon arrival, all offenders are required to complete the intake process. They must also undergo, or have undergone, a health screening evaluation, prior to taking part in any programming. Further, offenders complete an assessment to assist in the development of a case plan.

Three Program Segments

The aforementioned key factors are specified within three categories of options for offenders in the program. The program considers evidence-based practices and targets the risk of offenders to reoffend and offender needs based on program segments. Specifically, there are three segments: work restitution, work release, and work release/transition. Each segment is specifically designed to meet particular combined interventions of the eight principles of evidence-based programming and address the key program components as indicated above.

Work Restitution. Offenders in this segment of the program have the most restrictions and represent the highest level of risk to offend again. They participate exclusively on work crews. They are not allowed to move past RED status (most restrictive status for community movements) in the program and are not allowed social passes. They are not allowed movements within the community unless supervised by a staff member, but they can earn additional privileges within the facility as a result of positive behavior and adherence to program rules and case plan including progressing on goals and expectations. As well, at staff discretion, they may take part in a limited job search program on days when they are not participating on work crews, and if they obtain employment, thus lowering their risk to offend, they may move to the next segment of the program.

Work Release. Offenders in this segment of the program focus on maintaining and/or gaining employment in the community. Offenders have structured movements within the community with the sole purpose of gaining employment. There is an expectation that offenders become gainfully employed within a reasonable time period and maintain their employment. Through progress on meeting defined goals and expectations and positive behavior, offenders are allowed to move through the levels of the program and earn additional privileges. They are allowed to earn social pass time in the community to develop and strengthen family and community ties and to assist in their reintegration back to the community.

Work Release/Transition. Work release/transition is for offenders who have attained GREEN status (least restrictive status with respect to movements in the community) in the work release segment of the program, and/or who are in the program as a subsidy placement while transitioning into the community. Offenders are expected to be making, or have made, progress on defined goals and expectations. They must seek and/or maintain employment, actively participate in groups, maintain financial obligations, and assist other offenders who are starting out in the program. Additional privileges and social pass time are earned through positive behavior and adherence to program rules. . . .

In concert with best practice principles, and given the responsibility to operate effective and efficient programs, evaluation is an integral part of the program. An evaluation plan has been developed and will be implemented. The evaluation will measure short- and long-term outcomes based on the program model. . . .

What Is Restorative Justice?

Restorative justice is a theory of justice that emphasizes repairing the harm caused or revealed by criminal behaviour. . . .

Practices and programs reflecting restorative purposes will respond to crime by

1. identifying and taking steps to repair harm,
2. involving all stakeholders, and
3. transforming the traditional relationship between communities and their governments in responding to crime. . . .

Three principles form the foundation for restorative justice

1. Justice requires that we work to restore those who have been injured.
2. Those most directly involved and affected by crime should have the opportunity to participate fully . . . if they wish.
3. Government's role is to preserve a just public order, and the community's is to build and maintain a just peace.

Restorative programmes are characterized by four key values:

1. Encounter: Create opportunities for victims, offenders and community members who want to do so to meet to discuss the crime and its aftermath
2. Amends: Expect offenders to take steps to repair the harm they have caused
3. Reintegration: Seek to restore victims and offenders to whole, contributing members of society
4. Inclusion: Provide opportunities for parties with a stake in a specific crime to participate in its resolution

Restorative Justice Online,
"Introduction," Prison Fellowship International,
November 17, 2007. www.restorativejustice.org.

Measures were selected to assess both the short-term and long-term impact of the program. In general these include information about the offender's past, about the involvement in the program, about the accomplishments, and about performance following involvement.

There is no way to measure long-term outcomes in terms of achievements. However, short-term results include an increase of the number of offenders entering into treatment services. One hundred percent of all offenders entering into the program have been screened for substance abuse and cognitive restructuring. Of those indicating a need for treatment, 100 percent have engaged in the treatment process. This is much greater than the community engagement rate.

A few significant community partners have stepped up to assist in the program. Two key employers in the community are working with our agency to employ offenders in the work release component of the program. They have made more than 200 jobs available to offenders with a wide range of skill bases. Approximately 30 percent of offenders entering into the program have either found or maintained full-time employment. On the surface, this may not appear significant, but roughly only 35 percent have entered into the work release component of the program. This means that almost 86 percent of those that have been eligible to seek employment have been successful at obtaining employment prior to release from the program.

Various types of skills training have provided access to employment for offenders where it did not previously exist. One job assignment for work restitution (supervised work crews in the community) trains offenders to be firefighters. The program contracts with Oregon State Forestry and Bureau of Land Management to send crews out to fight fires. Upon completion of their sentences, many offenders have moved into employment with agencies contracted by the same parties.

In another instance, while participating in the program offenders have learned to prepare meals for large numbers of fellow offenders. This has been accomplished through job training in the program's kitchen facility. Many of these particular offenders have been able to transfer those skills to the community setting in positions of employment with various restaurants.

Alcohol and drug treatment, while in the early stages, has proved to be significant in terms of offenders remaining employable. One hundred percent of offenders entering the program have been assessed for alcohol and drug treatment needs. Of those indicated as needing treatment, 100 percent have entered into treatment programming. The rate of sobriety has increased significantly as compared to community placement. This has allowed some offenders the ability to maintain employment and sobriety as opposed to being incarcerated. The rate of positive urinalysis tests has decreased by 30 percent over the testing rate of offenders in the community not having participated in the program with an indicated need for treatment.

Recommendations for Future Changes

While the project is still in the early stages of implementation, I believe it is valuable to continue to implement the program as designed. It is founded on solid, evidence-based principles supported by research. It is important to follow through with the evaluation to ascertain whether or not the parallel research that drove the program design actually yields the desired outcomes.

It is also important to evaluate and determine whether or not the principles were applied as intended and supported by the research. It should be noted that although the design of the program is based upon evidence-based principles, the implementation of the program may not align with the manner in which those principles were intended to be implemented, and that could affect the outcomes regardless of design.

I would recommend the use of the Correctional Program Assessment Inventory (CPAI), or a similar measurement tool, to address the effectiveness of the program design and implementation, as opposed to solely basing findings on the program evaluation plan, which really focuses on outcomes. This would allow the program components to be "fine tuned" to potentially yield better outcomes and allow individual practices that align with evidence-based principles to be considered.

I would recommend reviewing the program components to better address the varied circumstances of the length of sentences for offenders participating in the program and adopt short-term measures that can measure short-term incremental change as opposed to only measuring long-term outcomes. This would allow the application of the definition of success at a lesser level and provide benchmarks with which to assess the program's viability in an ongoing manner. It would also provide a measurement for offenders participating in the program to allow time to realize individual success on a shorter-term basis.

> *"Sex offender treatment based on RPT has a moderate, but reliable, impact in reducing sex offender recidivism."*

Relapse Prevention Therapy Can Lower Recidivism Rates

George A. Parks

Relapse therapy is a series of psychological tools originally designed to help recovering alcoholics and drug addicts avoid resuming the use of harmful substances. In the following viewpoint, George A. Parks, the associate director of the Addictive Behaviors Research Center at the University of Washington, argues that this form of therapy can also be used to help reduce criminal recidivism. By working closely with individual offenders, corrections personnel can help them understand why they have committed crimes and what impact those crimes have had on others, which seem to be key components in preventing criminal relapse.

As you read, consider the following questions:

1. According to Craig Dowden, what three components make up the core of effective criminal relapse therapy?

2. What items are included in an offense scenario?

3. What are some examples of coaching strategies?

G. Alan Marlatt's cognitive-behavioral model of relapse prevention (RP), as described in his 1985 book co-edited with Judith R. Gordon [*Relapse Prevention*], was originally developed as a theory of alcohol relapse and a related set of intervention strategies designed to help clients who had completed treatment maintain abstinence by anticipating and coping with the problem of relapse. Soon after, the principles and practices of relapse prevention therapy (RPT) were applied to tobacco use, illicit drugs and addictive behaviors not related to substance abuse such as problem gambling, overeating and compulsive sexual behavior. A narrative review by [social science researchers] Kathleen Carroll and a meta-analysis by Jennifer E. Irvin and her colleagues concluded that RPT is an empirically supported treatment that is effective in the prevention and treatment of substance use disorders. The National Institute of Drug Abuse also classifies RPT as an evidence-based practice.

The increasing implementation of correctional programs based on RPT suggests that corrections professionals would benefit from a greater understanding of relapse and how relapse and criminal recidivism are related. While it was Marlatt and Gordon's 1985 book that stimulated correctional program development in the past 20 years, a 2005 revision and update of RPT by Marlatt and Donovan provides a contemporary review.

RPT in Corrections

Most corrections professionals are aware of the growing research evidence that rehabilitation programs based on cognitive-behavior therapy (CBT) are among the most effective treatments to reduce recidivism. So, it is not surprising that the flood of drug-involved offenders into correctional systems in the 1980s and the influence of the "what works" movement emphasizing evidence-based correctional practice led to the implementation of correctional programs based on RPT.

During the 1990s, both the U.S. Federal Bureau of Prisons (BOP) and the Correctional Service of Canada (CSC) developed, implemented and tested prison-based programs based on the RP model—the Residential Substance Abuse Treatment program in the U.S. and the Offender Substance Abuse Pre-Release Program in Canada. These programs utilized RPT as their treatment platform and as their source for specific cognitive-behavioral relapse prevention interventions. Evaluation research on the effectiveness of these offender substance abuse programs reviewed by Parks and Marlatt has demonstrated decreases in substance abuse relapse and criminal recidivism. The strongest treatment effects for RPT with substance abusing offenders occur when the in-prison substance abuse program is followed by continuing care in the community.

In the past 30 years, RPT has also become the dominant psychosocial treatment modality used in sex offender treatment programs, providing both the theoretical framework and specific strategies to reduce sex offense. In 1989, D. Richard Laws helped to launch the field of modern sex offender treatment with the publication of his book *Relapse Prevention with Sex Offenders*. In 2000, Laws and his colleagues provided a review of the applications of RPT to sex offenders and offered suggestions for remaking RPT to be more effective with this population. A recent review by Steve Aos and colleagues from the Washington State Institute for Public Policy concluded that sex offender treatment based on RPT has a moderate, but reliable, impact in reducing sex offender recidivism.

In 2003, Craig Dowden and his colleagues conducted a meta-analysis that provided an estimate of the overall impact of correctional programming based on RPT in reducing recidivism. They concluded that rehabilitation programs incorporating RPT consistently showed a moderate reduction in recidivism with larger recidivism reductions occurring when: there was a greater number of RPT core components; there was a more detailed description of the program; and the program targeted criminogenic needs. These three mediators of RPT program effectiveness demonstrate the importance of a cognitive-behavioral approach, focusing on program targets related to recidivism and a multimodal strategy using RPT core components in sufficient number and dosage to effect behavior change.

Dowden and his colleagues also identified several core components of RPT that reduced recidivism. The three most potent ingredients of RPT in offender programming are: 1) training significant others, including family and friends as well as spouses or girlfriends/boyfriends, in RP; 2) relapse rehearsal; and 3) conducting an offense chain analysis. Additional research is needed to identify more of RPT's significant components and the best way to combine these elements for greater impact in correctional programming.

Preventing Criminal Conduct

Traditional applications of RPT have been limited to rehabilitation programming for offenders who are already incarcerated or on probation and is primarily focused either on substance abuse or sex offending. In this section of the article, our attention will turn to contemporary approaches using RPT in corrections that apply the RP model in new and creative ways.

Recently, David Wexler has suggested that RPT could provide a model to promote crime reduction within the therapeutic jurisprudence framework by familiarizing criminal defense lawyers, prosecutors and judges with the RP model for their use during the adjudication process. Wexler argues that RPT can assist these officers of the court to collaboratively

RPT Core Components Used In Correctional Programs

- Train significant others in relapse prevention*
- Relapse rehearsal*
- Offense chain analysis*
- Identifying high-risk situations
- Coping skills training
- Booster session/aftercare
- Dealing with failure situations

* Designates strongest effect on criminal recidivism

George A. Parks,
"New Approaches to Using Relapse Prevention Therapy in the Criminal Justice System," Corrections Today, *December 2007.*

create recidivism prevention plans designed to help a defendant avoid, or cope with, high-risk scenarios for crime when living in the community on probation or after a period of incarceration. Wexler recommends that recidivism prevention plans developed within the RP model include victim input as well as the input and cooperation of the defendant and his or her family, friends, neighbors and other community members to create conditions to prevent recidivism that would then be ordered by the court and supervised by probation officers. Finally, Wexler observes that by engaging the offender and others in a thorough process of examining both the distal and proximal precursors of criminal conduct, both self-change and effective monitoring by others can be accomplished under the supervision of and with the support of the court.

In his recent paper on offender reentry, Jeremy Travis observes that the criminal justice system currently lacks an effective means to manage the reintegration of released offenders into the community and that traditional approaches to parole based solely on surveillance and sanctions have not reduced recidivism. Travis suggests that an innovative solution to this dilemma can be found in the RP model because a greater understanding of alcohol and drug relapse has the potential to stimulate the development of new strategies for offender risk management similar to the use of RPT for addictive behavior problems.

Travis suggests that reentry planning based on the RP model provides an alternative to the typical emphasis on "zero tolerance" in the criminal justice system by recognizing re-offense as an ongoing threat that requires proactive management by the offender, the community and the criminal justice system. Rather than automatically punishing an offender for re-offense or remanding him or her to custody, the RP model suggests that the occasion of criminal recidivism is an opportunity to debrief the incident, understand its predictable and controllable causes, and help the offender work harder and smarter at re-offense prevention with the support of the community and the court.

James McGuire echoes the sentiments expressed previously by Wexler and goes on to say "that the process of learning to avoid relapse . . . becomes a priority at the point of transition from institutions to the community . . ." At this point, there is a focus on parole decisions and formulating a release plan. He argues that offenders reentering the community must "acknowledge the existence of various problems, develop some understanding of how these are inter-connected with each other and . . . acquire new coping skills that will enable them to avoid re-offense."

McGuire further emphasizes that offender motivation to be aware of and prepare to cope with recidivism risk factors will be enhanced if the court and correctional officers use positive reinforcement to reward successful offender self-management. McGuire states that one implication of therapeutic jurisprudence is that research on offender rehabilitation, the therapeutic alliance, motivational enhancement and relapse prevention should not "remain confined to the domain of social science when they have the capacity to illuminate offending behavior and inform legal responses to it." He states further. "By capitalizing on what we now know about offender treatment and personal change, such a development could maximize the therapeutic benefit of legal decisions?"

Other RPT Administrators

John A. Cunningham and his colleagues describe another innovative application of RPT based on a related cognitive-behavioral model of relapse called structured relapse prevention (SRP), developed by Helen Annis in her seminal studies of relapse conducted at the Addiction Research Foundation in Toronto. SRP is an outpatient program that combines motivational enhancement strategies and cognitive-behavioral interventions. A field test of SRP delivered by probation and parole officers was conducted in Ontario, Canada to assess the feasibility and effectiveness of this approach. Ten probation and parole officers were trained to deliver SRP and provided the SRP program to 55 offenders during a one-year period. The SRP protocol was modified for use in probation, and correctional officers were readily able to learn and apply the model in the supervision of their offenders.

Probation officers delivering the program commented on the common-sense appeal of the SRP model and found it easy to use. They also said it was sometimes a welcome alternative for offenders who were resistant to attending substance abuse treatment. While it was difficult for the probation officers to integrate delivering SRP into their other duties, overall they reported they would recommend the implementation of SRP, The authors note, "On the basis of the field test results, the Ontario Ministry of the Solicitor General and Correctional

Services recommended dissemination of SRP to Probation and Parole Officers throughout the province."

For many years Canadian criminologist Edward Zamble has been asking, "How do we make community supervision more effective?" As a result of his research on the coping deficiencies of offenders and the recidivism process, Zamble came to the conclusion that the greatest limitation in current supervision practices is that "they lack a coherent theoretical justification or rationale." He also speculated that a theoretical account of the recidivism process based on the RP model could provide corrections professionals with guidelines for offender monitoring and more effective supervision strategies in order to "identify the proximal antecedents to criminal recidivism generally ... [and to] tell a supervising officer what the signs are that a given offender is about to commit a new offense."

Zamble discovered the major difference between recidivists and nonrecidivists was not the amount of stress or problems they were exposed to or the severity of their past crimes but rather the way they interpreted and responded to external events and their internal states. He further suggested that recidivism was typically preceded by an observable pattern of precursors and seemed to vary predictably depending on offender characteristics and the type of crime committed. Zamble observed that much like alcohol and drug relapse, criminal recidivism is the result of a breakdown process, and the causes of recidivism are distinct from those that may have caused the original crimes to occur. Labeling this theory the coping-relapse model of criminal recidivism. Zamble and his colleagues describe recidivism as beginning with a learned propensity to commit crimes evoked by stressful life events whose impact is worsened by inadequate coping skills. This leads to compensatory responses such as substance abuse, anti-social thinking, seeking anti-social associates and, finally, committing crimes consistent with the person's past repertoire of criminal behaviors.

Noting the critical point for effective supervision, Zamble says, "These emotions and thoughts are identifiable, distinctive, and characteristic of offenders in similar circumstances. [Further that] the model hypothesizes that the psychological precursors of recidivism 'would be visible to an objective observer ... That outside observer could be the parole officer, acting in a redefined role ... [to] monitor the verified antecedents of recidivism." Finally, Zamble says that if the antecedents or precursors of recidivism could be identified in a given case then perhaps the offender, the parole officer and the offender's significant others could create a checklist of warning signs leading to recidivism and intervene in appropriate ways to prevent the occurrence of a new offense when any of the warning signs begin to appear.

RPT as a Case Management Tool

The author and his colleagues have been attempting to create an RPT case management tool to move from the more general statement of the coping-relapse model of recidivism proposed by Zamble to the specific application of RPT in community supervision. In order to use RPT as a case management tool for a given offender, the corrections professional must first complete a detailed assessment used to create a criminal behavior profile that contains three elements: crime cycles consisting of all known offense scenarios; offense scenarios describing all crimes or crime types committed in the past; and offense chain pathways that lead step-by-step to the offense scenarios. The criminal behavior profile forms the basis for a recidivism prevention plan created in collaboration with the offender to be used by the offender, his or her significant others, and the correctional officer to monitor recidivism risk and intervene accordingly.

Crime cycles consist of the repertoire of offenses that have occurred repeatedly in an offender's criminal history. Each of these crime cycles occurs under a specific and predictable set of conditions called offense scenarios. Offense scenarios include the "who, what, how, with whom, to whom, when, where and why" of each crime cycle. In order to create offense scenarios, specific information is required for each offense or a sufficient number of similar offenses. This specific information is gathered both through a file review of criminal records and an interview with the offender. Part of the offender interview is also used to identify the last component of the profile, the offense chain pathways that lead the offender step-by-step toward new acts of criminal behavior, which are likely to occur during exposure to an offense scenario where committing a crime is difficult to avoid.

The key to using RPT for recidivism prevention is to know an offender's crime cycles and their associated offense scenarios and offense chain pathways by conducting a thorough functional analysis of the distal and proximal precursors to offense. Intervening early in the process, before exposure to the offense scenario, can prevent a crime from occurring. However, it is not possible for an offender to avoid all offense scenarios, so offenders must also learn how to escape these offense scenarios or cope with them without committing a crime.

In an RPT-driven case management process, corrections professionals, the offender, and his or her significant others will use this functional analysis of criminal conduct consisting of crime cycles, offense scenarios and cognitive-behavioral offense chain pathways to prevent recidivism (i.e., as a checklist of warning signs). As a corrections professional gets a better picture of the circumstances that trigger recidivism by understanding the chain of events leading to offense scenarios, he or she can prevent crimes by using "coaching strategies" that improve an offender's coping skills such as teaching offenders how to better identify high-risk offense scenarios and to develop strategies to avoid them or escape them without committing a crime. A corrections professional can also use "catching strategies" that intervene to prevent crimes through surveillance and incapacitation such as increased monitoring, more frequent office contacts, and field visits at the offender's home or work.

While these new applications of the RP model offer corrections evidence-based interventions designed to reduce recidivism, much work remains to be done in refining and applying RPT beyond its traditional role in offender programming. Hopefully, correctional innovations based on RPT will continue to be developed, disseminated and tested to further the goals of crime reduction and successful integration of offenders into the community. The most important contributions of the RP model to the criminal justice system may be found in its implications for a philosophy of human nature that optimistically states that people can and do change and that crimes may be viewed as behaviors enacted by people, not traits forever defining them.

Periodical Bibliography

The following articles have been selected to supplement the diverse views presented in this chapter.

Hal Arkowitz and Scott O. Lilienfeld	"Misunderstood Crimes," *Scientific American Mind*, vol. 19, no. 2, 2008.
Hannah Beech	"Prison Break," *Time Atlantic*, June 30, 2008.
Art Beeler	"Let's Spend Second Chance Money Wisely," *Corrections Today*, October 2008.
Rose Marie Berger and Jeannie Choi	"A Broken System," *Sojourners Magazine*, February 2009.
Francina C. Carter	"Offender Employment Is the Key," *Corrections Today*, August 2008.
Economist	"Killing for Respect," vol. 390, no. 8626, April 11, 2009.
Harriet Hall	"Hope for Reentering the Community," *Behavioral Healthcare*, March 2008.
Richard Rosenfeld, Joan Petersilia, and Christy Visher	"The First Days After Release Can Make a Difference," *Corrections Today*, June 2008.
Daa'iya L. Sanusi	"Correctional Education Reduces Recidivism," *New York Amsterdam News*, February 19, 2009.
Justine Sharrock	"The Shawnee Redemption," *Mother Jones*, July/August 2008.
Suzanne Smalley and Arian Campo-Flores	"A Downward Spiral," *Newsweek*, November 11, 2007.
Linda Zundel	"Pathways Reentry Program: Connecting with Our Community for Change Success," *American Jails*, March/April 2009.

For Further Discussion

Chapter 1

1. Richard F. Doyle and the Correctional Association of New York discuss whether the justice system treats men and women fairly. After reading their viewpoints, do you think that the justice system is biased against either gender? Why or why not?

2. What evidence does Nicole Summer use to prove that women are vulnerable in prison? What evidence does Daniel Brook use to prove that men are vulnerable in prison? Whose viewpoint do you find most convincing, and why?

3. Leadership Conference on Civil Rights Education Fund and the New Century Foundation's viewpoints are in response to recent controversies about racist stereotyping by police officers and the criminal justice system. Based on the evidence each author provides, do you think police officers unfairly target minorities? Why or why not?

Chapter 2

1. Barry Holman, in his interview with *Justice Matters*, argues that elderly prisoners should be released early. Kelly Porcella argues that elderly criminals should not be given special consideration during sentencing. After reading these two viewpoints, do you think elderly criminals should be treated differently by the criminal justice system? Why or why not?

2. Richard E. Vatz and the American Civil Liberties Union debate the culpability of mentally ill offenders. Which viewpoint offers the strongest evidence? Explain your answer.

3. Rob Norton argues that due to the nature of the crime, white-collar criminals should be given lighter sentences. Ming Zhen Shakya argues that white-collar criminals do not deserve special treatment. Which viewpoint is more convincing? Why?

Chapter 3

1. David B. Muhlhausen argues that the death penalty deters crime. Aundré M. Herron argues that it does not. Based on the evidence offered, do you think the death penalty deters crime? Why or why not?

2. Spencer E. Ante argues that surveillance equipment helps deter crime. Based on the evidence he provides, can you describe how these devices might work? Or do you agree with the American Civil Liberties Union, which asserts that surveillance devices not only fail to prevent crime, but also invade privacy?

Chapter 4

1. According to Martha Lyman and Stefan LoBuglio, why is measuring recidivism so difficult? Can you think of ways that researchers might measure recidivism?

2. The Government Accountability Office argues that rehabilitation can be an effective tool for reducing the recidivism rates of drug offenders, George A. Parks argues that relapse prevention therapy is an effective means of deterring future criminal offenses, and Danny L. Jordan argues that transition programs are the answer. In what ways do these approaches differ? Which viewpoint is more persuasive? Explain your answer.

3. Jason Newman argues that corrections officials should be held responsible for criminal recidivism. Based on his evidence, do you agree? If not, who should be held responsible for criminals committing future crimes?

4. What evidence does Jonathan Aitken use to argue that restorative justice is better than retribution in reducing recidivism? Based on the evidence provided, do you agree? Why or why not?

Organizations to Contact

The editors have compiled the following list of organizations concerned with the issues debated in this book. The descriptions are derived from materials provided by the organizations. All have publications or information available for interested readers. The list was compiled on the date of publication of the present volume; the information provided here may change. Be aware that many organizations take several weeks or longer to respond to inquiries, so allow as much time as possible.

American Civil Liberties Union (ACLU)
915 Fifteenth Street NW, Washington, DC   20005
(202) 393-4930 • fax: (757) 563-1655
e-mail: wso@al-anon.org
Web site: www.aclu.org

The American Civil Liberties Union (ACLU) is a national organization that works to defend Americans' civil rights as guaranteed by the U.S. Constitution. It opposes curfew laws for juveniles and seeks to protect the right of gang members to assemble in public. Among the ACLU's numerous publications are the book *In Defense of American Liberties: A History of the ACLU*, the handbook *The Rights of Prisoners: A Comprehensive Guide to the Legal Rights of Prisoners Under Current Law*, and the briefing paper "Crime and Civil Liberties."

Bureau of Justice Statistics (BJS)
810 Seventh Street NW, Washington, DC   20531
(202) 307-0765
e-mail: askbjs@usdoj.gov
Web site: www.ojp.usdoj.gov

The mission of the Bureau of Justice Statistics (BJS) is to collect, analyze, publish, and disseminate information on crime, criminal offenders, victims of crime, and the operation of justice systems at all levels of government. This data is critical to federal, state, and local policy makers in combating crime and ensuring that justice is both efficient and evenhanded. BJS's Web site offers a clearinghouse of statistics from all areas of criminal justice.

Cato Institute

1000 Massachusetts Avenue NW, Washington, DC 20001
(202) 842-0200 • fax: (202) 842-3490
e-mail: cato@cato.org
Web site: www.cato.org

The Cato Institute is a libertarian public policy research foundation. It evaluates government policies and offers reform proposals in its publication *Policy Analysis*. Topics include "Crime, Police, and Root Causes" and "Prison Blues: How America's Foolish Sentencing Policies Endanger Public Safety." In addition, the institute publishes the bimonthly newsletter *Cato Policy Report* and the triannual *Cato Journal*.

Center for Research on Youth and Social Policy (CRYSP)

University of Pennsylvania School of Social Work
Philadelphia, PA 19104-6179
(215) 898-2229 • fax: (215) 573-2791
e-mail: crysp@sp2.upenn.edu
Web site: www.sp2.upenn.edu

The Center for Research on Youth and Social Policy (CRYSP) works to bring about positive social change by improving the way human services are developed, delivered, and evaluated. CRYSP seeks to have a major impact on the issues and systems affecting vulnerable populations, particularly children, while promoting social justice and social change through applied research, planning, and technical assistance. It publishes the booklets *Home-Based Services for Serious and Violent Juvenile Offenders, Youth Violence: An Overview,* and *Meditation Involving Juveniles: Ethical Dilemmas and Policy Questions.*

The Heritage Foundation
214 Massachusetts Avenue NE, Washington, DC   20002
(202) 546-4400 • fax: (202) 546-8328
e-mail: info@heritage.org
Web site: www.heritage.org

The Heritage Foundation is a conservative public policy research institute. It advocates tougher sentencing and the construction of more prisons as means to reduce crime. The foundation publishes the quarterly journal *Policy Review,* which occasionally contains articles addressing juvenile crime.

Innocence Project
100 Fifth Avenue, 3rd Floor, New York, NY   10011
(212) 364-5340
e-mail: info@innocentproject.org
Web site: www.innocenceproject.org

The Innocence Project is a nonprofit legal clinic affiliated with the Benjamin N. Cardozo School of Law at Yeshiva University and created by Barry C. Scheck and Peter J. Neufeld in 1992. The project is a national litigation and public policy organization dedicated to exonerating wrongfully convicted people through DNA testing and reforming the criminal justice system to prevent future injustice. The Innocence Project regularly publishes facts sheets such as "Facts on Post-Conviction DNA Exonerations" and the newsletter *The Innocence Project in Print.*

Justice Fellowship
44180 Riverside Parkway, Lansdowne, VA   20176
(703) 904-7312 • fax: (703) 478-9679
Web site: www.pfm.org

The Justice Fellowship is a national justice reform organization that advocates victims' rights, alternatives to prison, and community involvement in the criminal justice system. It aims to make the criminal justice system more consistent with biblical teachings on justice. It publishes the brochures *A Case for Victims' Rights* and *Beyond Crime and Punishment: Restorative Justice* and the quarterly newsletter *Justice Report*.

Milton S. Eisenhower Foundation
1875 Connecticut Avenue NW, Suite 410
Washington, DC   20009
(202) 234-8104
e-mail: info@eisenhowerfoundation.org
Web site: www.eisenhowerfoundation.org

The Milton S. Eisenhower Foundation consists of individuals dedicated to reducing crime in inner-city neighborhoods through community programs. It believes that more federally funded programs such as Head Start and Job Corps would improve education and job opportunities for youths, thus reducing juvenile crime and violence. The foundation's publications include the report "To Establish Justice, To Insure Domestic Tranquility: A Thirty-Year Update of the National Commission on the Causes and Prevention of Violence" and the book *Youth Investment and Police Mentoring*.

National Association of Blacks in Criminal Justice (NABCJ)
North Carolina Central University, Durham, NC   27707
(919) 683-1801 • fax: (919) 683-1903
Web site: www.nabcj.org

Founded in 1972, the National Association of Blacks in Criminal Justice (NABCJ) includes criminal justice professionals concerned with the impact of criminal justice policies and practices on the minority community. It seeks to increase the influence of blacks in the judicial system. Publications include the quarterly *NABCJ Newsletter* and the bimonthly newsletter *The Commitment*.

National Center on Institutions and Alternatives (NCIA)
3125 Mt. Vernon Avenue, Alexandria, VA   22305
(703) 684-0373 • fax: (703) 684-6037

e-mail: ncia@igc.apc.org
Web site: www.ncianet.org

The National Center on Institutions and Alternatives (NCIA) works to reduce the number of people institutionalized in prisons and mental hospitals. It favors the least restrictive forms of detention for juvenile offenders and opposes sentencing juveniles as adults and executing juvenile murderers. NCIA publishes the study *Darkness Closes In—National Study of Jail Suicides* and offers the book *The Real War on Crime,* published by HarperCollins.

National Council on Crime and Delinquency (NCCD)
1970 Broadway, Suite 500, Oakland, CA   94612
(510) 208-0500
Web site: www.nccd-crc.org

The National Council on Crime and Delinquency (NCCD) is composed of corrections specialists and others interested in the juvenile justice system and the prevention of crime and delinquency. It advocates community-based treatment programs rather than imprisonment for delinquent youths. It opposes placing minors in adult jails and executing those who commit capital offenses before the age of eighteen. The NCCD publishes the quarterly *Crime and Delinquency* and policy papers "Juvenile Justice Policy Statement" and "Unlocking Juvenile Corrections: Evaluating the Massachusetts Department of Youth Services."

National Crime Prevention Council (NCPC)
1700 K Street NW, 2nd Floor, Washington, DC   20006-3817
(202) 466-6272 • fax: (202) 296-1356
Web site: www.ncpc.org

The National Crime Prevention Council (NCPC) advocates job training and recreation programs as means to reduce youth crime and violence. The council provides training and technical assistance to groups and individuals interested in crime prevention and sponsors the Take a Bite Out of Crime campaign. It publishes the book *Preventing Violence: Program Ideas and Examples,* the booklet *How Communities Can Bring Up Youth Free from Fear and Violence,* and the newsletter *Catalyst,* which is published ten times a year.

National Criminal Justice Association (NCJA)
444 North Capitol Street NW, Suite 618
Washington, DC   20001
(202) 347-4900 • fax: (202) 508-3859
e-mail: info@ncja.org
Web site: www.ncja.org

The National Criminal Justice Association (NCJA) is an association of state and local police chiefs, judges, attorneys, and other criminal justice officials that seeks to improve the administration of state criminal and juvenile justice programs. It publishes the monthly newsletter *Justice Bulletin.*

National Institute of Justice (NIJ)
PO Box 6000, Rockville, MD   20849-6000
(800) 851-3420 • fax: (301) 519-5212
e-mail: askncjrs@ncjrs.org
Web site: www.ncjrs.org

The National Institute of Justice (NIJ) is a research and development agency that documents crime and its control. It publishes and distributes information through the National Criminal Justice Reference Service, an international clearinghouse that provides information and research about criminal justice. NIJ publications include the bimonthly *National Institute of Justice Journal.*

The Sentencing Project
514 Tenth Street NW, Suite 1000, Washington, DC   20004
(202) 628-0871 • fax: 202-628-1091
e-mail: staff@sentencingproject.org
Web site: www.sentencingproject.org

The Sentencing Project provides public defenders and other public officials with information on establishing and improving alternative sentencing programs that provide convicted persons with positive and constructive options to incarceration. It promotes increased public understanding of the sentencing process and alternative sentencing programs. It publishes the reports "Americans Behind Bars: A Comparison of International Rates of Incarceration," "Americans Behind Bars: One Year Later," and "Young Black Men and the Criminal Justice System: A Growing National Problem."

Violence Policy Center (VPC)
1730 Rhode Island Avenue NW, Suite 1014
Washington, DC   20036
(202) 822-8200
e-mail: info@vpc.org
Web site: www.vpc.org

The Violence Policy Center (VPC) is an educational foundation that conducts research on firearms violence. It works to educate the public concerning the dangers of guns and supports gun-control measures. The center's publications include the reports "Safe at Home: How DC's Gun Laws Save Children's Lives" and "Really Big Guns, Even Bigger Lies."

Youth Crime Watch of America (YCWA)
9200 South Dadeland Boulevard, Suite 417, Miami, FL   33156
(305) 670-2409
e-mail: ycwa@ycwa.org
Web site: www.ycwa.org

Youth Crime Watch of America (YCWA) is dedicated to establishing Youth Crime Watch programs across the United States. It strives to give youths the tools and guidance necessary to actively reduce crime and drug use in their schools and communities. Its publications include *Talking to Youth About Crime Prevention*, the workbook *Community Based Youth Crime Watch Program Handbook*, and the motivational video *Put An End to School Violence Today.*

Bibliography of Books

Gregg Barak, Paul Leighton, and Jeanne Flavin
Class, Race, Gender, and Crime: The Social Realities of Justice in America. Lanham, MD: Rowman and Littlefield Publishers, 2007.

Michael Benson
White-Collar Crime. New York: Chelsea House, 2008.

Michael Dow Burkhead
The Treatment of Criminal Offenders: A History. Jefferson, NC: McFarland, 2007.

Paul Cromwell, ed.
In Their Own Words: Criminals on Crime. New York: Oxford University Press, 2006.

Madoka Futamura
War Crimes Tribunals and Transitional Justice: The Tokyo Trial and the Nuremburg Legacy. New York: Routledge, 2008.

Phyllis B. Gerstenfeld, ed.
Crime and Punishment in the United States. Pasadena, CA: Salem Press, 2008.

David Givens
Crime Signals: How to Spot a Criminal Before You Become a Victim. New York: St. Martin's Press, 2008.

Frank E. Hagan
Crime Types and Criminals. Thousand Oaks, CA: Sage Publications, 2009.

Steve Hall, Simon Winlow, and Craig Ancrum
Criminal Identities and Consumer Culture: Crime, Exclusion and the New Culture of Narcissism. Portland, OR: Willan, 2008.

Christopher Harding
Criminal Enterprise: Individuals, Organisations and Criminal Responsibility. Portland, OR: Willan, 2007.

Rob Hornsby and Dick Hobbs, eds.
Gun Crime. Burlington, VT: Ashgate, 2008.

Human Rights Watch
Targeting Blacks: Drug Law Enforcement and Race in the United States. New York: Human Rights Watch, 2008.

Radha Iyengar
I'd Rather Be Hanged for a Sheep than a Lamb: The Unintended Consequences of "Three-Strikes" Laws. Cambridge, MA: National Bureau of Economic Research, 2008.

Rolf Loeber, ed.
Tomorrow's Criminals: The Development of Child Delinquency and Effective Interventions. Burlington, VT: Ashgate, 2008.

Michael J. Lynch
Big Prisons, Big Dreams: Crime and the Failure of America's Penal System. New Brunswick, NJ: Rutgers University Press, 2007.

Doris Layton
Mackenzie
Different Crimes Different Criminals: Understanding, Treating and Preventing Criminal Behavior. Newark, NJ: Anderson Publishing/LexisNexis, 2006.

Mike Mayo
American Murder: Criminals, Crime, and the Media. Canton, MI: Visible Ink Press, 2008.

Carlo Morselli
Inside Criminal Networks. New York: Springer Science and Business Media, 2009.

Michael Newton
Celebrities and Crime. New York: Chelsea House, 2008.

Katheryn
Russell-Brown
The Color of Crime. New York: New York University Press, 2009.

Joanne Savage,
ed.
The Development of Persistent Criminality. New York: Oxford University Press, 2009.

Frank R. Scarpitti,
Amie L. Nielsen,
and J. Mitchell
Miller, eds.
Crime and Criminals: Contemporary and Classic Readings in Criminology, 2nd ed. New York: Oxford University Press, 2009.

Robert W. Taylor
Digital Crime and Digital Terrorism. Upper Saddle River, NJ: Pearson Prentice Hall, 2006.

Katherine Stuart
van Wormer and
Clemens Bartollas
Women and the Criminal Justice System. Boston, MA: Pearson Allyn and Bacon, 2007.

Bruce N. Waller   *You Decide! Current Debates in Criminal Justice.* Upper Saddle River, NJ: Pearson Prentice Hall, 2009.

John Paul Wright,   *Criminals in the Making: Criminality Across the Life Course.* Los Angeles: Sage, 2008.
Stephen G.
Tibbetts, and
Leah E. Daigle

Index